Frommer's®

Los Angeles
day BY **day**

1st Edition

by Garth Mueller

WILEY

Wiley Publishing, Inc.

Contents

Published by:

Wiley Publishing, Inc.

111 River St.
Hoboken, NJ 07030-5774

ISBN 978-0-470-19081-4
Editor: Cate Latting
Special thanks to Margot Weiss
Production Editor: Suzanna R. Thompson
Photo Editor: Richard Fox
Cartographer: Roberta Stockwell
Production by Wiley Indianapolis Composition Services

For information on our other products and services or to obtain technical
support, please contact our Customer Care Department within the U.S.
at 800/762-2974, outside the U.S. at 317/572-3993 or fax 317/572-4002.

Wiley also publishes its books in a variety of electronic formats. Some
content that appears in print may not be available in electronic formats.

Manufactured in China

5   4   3   2   1

A Note from the Publisher

Organizing your time. That's what this guide is all about.

Other guides give you long lists of things to see and do and then expect you to fit the pieces together. The Day by Day guides are different. These guides tell you the best of everything, and then they show you how to see it *in the smartest, most time-efficient way*. Our authors have designed detailed itineraries organized by time, neighborhood, or special interest. And each tour comes with a bulleted map that takes you from stop to stop.

Hoping to tour Hollywood's famous sights, stroll Venice Beach, or shop your way through all of L.A.? Planning a walk through downtown, or plotting a day of fun-filled activities with the kids? Whatever your interest or schedule, the Day by Days give you the smartest routes to follow. Not only do we take you to the top attractions, hotels, and restaurants, but we also help you access those special moments that locals get to experience—those "finds" that turn tourists into travelers.

The Day by Days are also your top choice if you're looking for one complete guide for all your travel needs. The best hotels and restaurants for every budget, the greatest shopping values, the wildest nightlife—it's all here.

Why should you trust our judgment? Because our authors personally visit each place they write about. They're an independent lot who say what they think and would never include places they wouldn't recommend to their best friends. They're also open to suggestions from readers. If you'd like to contact them, please send your comments my way at mspring@wiley.com, and I'll pass them on.

Enjoy your Day by Day guide—the most helpful travel companion you can buy. And have the trip of a lifetime.

Warm regards,

Michael Spring, Publisher
Frommer's Travel Guides

About the Author

Garth Mueller was born in northern California, but it took him 27 years to make it south to Los Angeles, where he's resided for the past 10 years. He has written and produced several award-winning short films, and has sold a screenplay, *King of the Space-Age Bachelor Pad,* to Fox Searchlight Pictures. He holds a B.A. in English from Emory University and an M.F.A. in film production from Florida State University.

Acknowledgments

For my extraordinary wife, Barb Crawford—home is wherever you are.

Loads of thanks to my editor, Cate Latting, for the opportunity to rediscover my city, and for rescuing me when I fell into its rabbit holes.

An Additional Note

Please be advised that travel information is subject to change at any time— and this is especially true of prices. We therefore suggest that you write or call ahead for confirmation when making your travel plans. The authors, editors, and publisher cannot be held responsible for the experiences of readers while traveling. Your safety is important to us, however, so we encourage you to stay alert and be aware of your surroundings.

Star Ratings, Icons & Abbreviations

Every hotel, restaurant, and attraction listing in this guide has been ranked for quality, value, service, amenities, and special features using a **star-rating system.** Hotels, restaurants, attractions, shopping, and nightlife are rated on a scale of zero stars (recommended) to three stars (exceptional). In addition to the star-rating system, we also use a **kids icon** to point out the best bets for families. Within each tour, we recommend cafes, bars, or restaurants where you can take a break. Each of these stops appears in a shaded box marked with a coffee-cup-shaped bullet ☕.

The following **abbreviations** are used for credit cards:

AE	American Express	DISC	Discover	V	Visa
DC	Diners Club	MC	MasterCard		

Frommers.com

Now that you have this guidebook to help you plan a great trip, visit our website at **www.frommers.com** for additional travel information on more than 3,600 destinations. We update features regularly to give you instant access to the most current trip-planning information available. At Frommers.com, you'll find scoops on the best airfares, lodging rates, and car rental bargains. You can even book your travel online through our reliable travel booking partners. Other popular features include:

- Online updates of our most popular guidebooks
- Vacation sweepstakes and contest giveaways
- Newsletters highlighting the hottest travel trends
- Online travel message boards with featured travel discussions

A Note on Prices

In the "Take a Break" and "Best Bets" sections of this book, we have used a system of dollar signs to show a range of costs for 1 night in a hotel (the price of a double-occupancy room) or the cost of an entree at a restaurant. Use the following table to decipher the dollar signs:

Cost	Hotels	Restaurants
$	under $150	under $10
$$	$150–$250	$10–$20
$$$	$250–$350	$20–$30
$$$$	$350–$450	$30–$40
$$$$$	over $450	over $40

An Invitation to the Reader

In researching this book, we discovered many wonderful places—hotels, restaurants, shops, and more. We're sure you'll find others. Please tell us about them, so we can share the information with your fellow travelers in upcoming editions. If you were disappointed with a recommendation, we'd love to know that, too. Please write to:

Frommer's Los Angeles Day by Day, 1st Edition
Wiley Publishing, Inc. • 111 River St. • Hoboken, NJ 07030-5774

15 Favorite
Moments

15 Favorite **Moments**

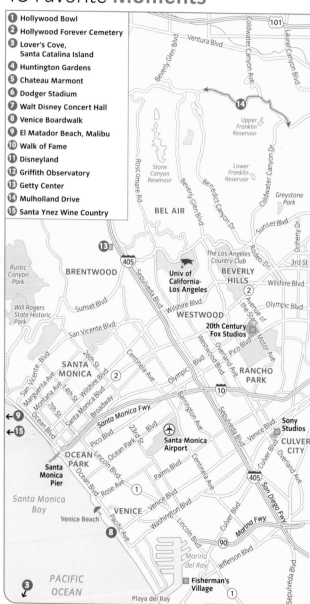

1 Hollywood Bowl
2 Hollywood Forever Cemetery
3 Lover's Cove, Santa Catalina Island
4 Huntington Gardens
5 Chateau Marmont
6 Dodger Stadium
7 Walt Disney Concert Hall
8 Venice Boardwalk
9 El Matador Beach, Malibu
10 Walk of Fame
11 Disneyland
12 Griffith Observatory
13 Getty Center
14 Mulholland Drive
15 Santa Ynez Wine Country

Previous page: Architect Frank Gehry's Walt Disney Concert Hall.

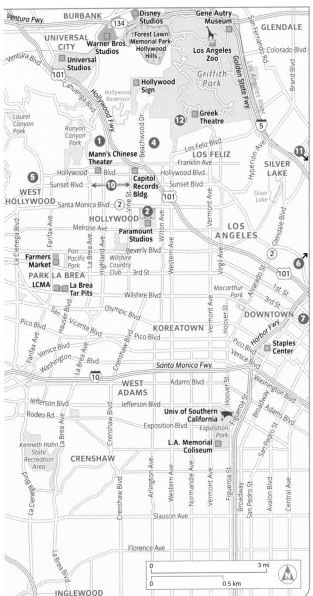

Constantly adapting to new identities, Los Angeles is a great actor, impossible to pin down. I love the way that, within a single block, the city can switch from gritty to glitzy, capable of embodying both the American Dream of endless opportunity ("Go west, young man") and the American Nightmare of not being cool enough ("You're not on the guest list, man"). Here's a highlight reel of some of L.A.'s best roles, from star-making turns to bit parts.

① Pack a picnic for the Hollywood Bowl. The nation's largest natural amphitheater is a lovely place to enjoy dinner with a bottle of wine under the stars. Summer home to the L.A. Philharmonic, the Bowl also hosts touring heavyweights like Willie Nelson and Radiohead. *See p 130.*

② Catch a flick at the Hollywood Forever Cemetery. Join Rudolph Valentino, Douglas Fairbanks, and the other unemployed actors here any Saturday night in summer. You can spread a blanket, rest your head against a headstone, and enjoy the show, usually something classic and creepy. And feel free to scream— you won't wake anybody. *See p 48.*

③ Snorkel in Lover's Cove. This marine preserve on Santa Catalina Island is only 22 miles from the mainland. If you're looking for an urban escape, this should float your boat. The water is calm, blue, and dotted with colorful schools of small fish such as calico bass, blue perch, and the neon-orange garibaldi, California's protected state fish. *See p 160.*

④ Stop and smell the roses in the Huntington Botanical Gardens. The Rose Garden is my favorite among these 150 green acres, which manage to appear both manicured and sprawling. Applaud nature's sense of humor in some of the strange, ballooning succulents of the Desert Garden, or Zen out in the quiet retreat of the Japanese Garden. *See p 96.*

⑤ Soak up some Old Hollywood glamour with your highball. The lobby of the infamous Chateau Marmont may be a costly place for a cocktail, but it buys you a chance to stargaze on the sly. This legendary hideaway prides itself on its exclusivity; to gain entry, you'll need either a globally recognized face or a hard-won reservation at the hotel or restaurant. *See p 143.*

⑥ Down a Dodger Dog. Dodger Stadium welcomed the boys from Brooklyn back in 1962. While newer sports stadiums strain to manufacture a vintage vibe, Dodger Stadium is a SoCal classic, sunny and laidback, with swaying palm trees framing panoramic views of the San Gabriel Mountains and Downtown. *See p 133.*

The tearoom overlooks the Rose Garden at the Huntington Botanical Gardens.

An in-line skater draws a crowd on the Venice Boardwalk.

7 Experience the majesty of the Walt Disney Concert Hall. This is the other home of the L.A. Philharmonic (those lucky dogs). Frank Gehry's audacious exterior looks gift-wrapped by God in curvilinear steel, a stunning catalyst for the revitalization of Downtown. But the hall is no hollow shell—the acoustics within are flawless. A must-see and a must-hear. See p 130.

8 Rollerblade up Venice Boardwalk. C'mon, there's no shame in trying. Matter of fact, there's no shame in anything on this kitschy stretch of street performers, leathery-skinned exhibitionists, tacky trinket peddlers, break dancers, soothsayers, and doomsayers. If you've got a freak flag, this is the spot to fly it. See p 60.

9 Tiptoe in the tide pools. Pick the right time—early on weekdays, off-season—to explore the rocky coves of El Matador Beach, a remote enclave backed against the cliffs of Malibu, and, with a little luck, you'll get what many locals hold so dear—a little privacy. See p 85.

10 Walk the Walk of Fame. The front of Grauman's Chinese Theatre may be crawling with tourists, but hey, aren't you one of them? Snap a couple of shots of you posing with an out-of-shape Superman or an ill-tempered Marilyn Monroe, but draw the line at boarding a tour bus of star homes. See p 10.

11 Smash the space-time continuum. Rocket through the black void of Space Mountain in Disneyland—if you dare. Just because they call it "The Happiest Place on Earth" doesn't mean it can't scare the bejeezus out of you. Swear you'll never do that again, breathe, and get back in line. See p 152.

Famous film stars leave their marks outside Grauman's Chinese Theatre.

The Griffith Observatory reopened in 2006 after a $93-million renovation.

⓬ **Celebrate some lesser-known stars.** At the newly renovated Griffith Observatory, it's easy to get caught up in the scientific exhibits, the planetarium, or the spectacular views of the city and the HOLLYWOOD

Van Gogh's Irises *is one of the Getty Center's main attractions.*

sign, but don't forget to direct some of that wonder skyward. Mounted on both copper domes are telescopes, free for public use, to help us (in the words of the park's benefactor Griffith J. Griffith) broaden our human perspective. *See p 93.*

⓭ **Get sketchy at the Getty Center.** Feast your eyes on Monet's Impressionistic gems or on *Irises* by Vincent van Gogh, and once you're sufficiently inspired, head over to the sketching gallery, where you can try your hand at mimicking the masters. *See p 11.*

⓮ **Cruise Mulholland Drive.** A great way to get the lay of the land is to drive the winding ridgeline of the Santa Monica Mountains, which separates the city from the valley. Pull off onto one of the many overlooks for stunning panoramas. *See p 13.*

⓯ **Explore the wine country.** Sample the pinot noirs and chardonnays at one of many wineries nestled among the rolling hills of vineyards in the Santa Ynez Valley north of Santa Barbara. *See p 162.* ●

1 The Best Full-Day Tours

The Best **in One Day**

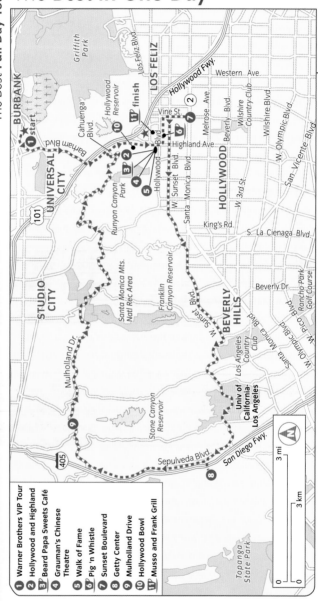

1. Warner Brothers VIP Tour
2. Hollywood and Highland
3. Beard Papa Sweets Café
4. Grauman's Chinese Theatre
5. Walk of Fame
6. Pig 'n Whistle
7. Sunset Boulevard
8. Getty Center
9. Mulholland Drive
10. Hollywood Bowl
11. Musso and Frank Grill

Previous page: All first-time visitors to L.A. should take a drive on Sunset Boulevard.

Seeing the country's largest city in a single day takes preparation. It's best to secure reservations in advance for the Warner Brothers VIP tour, your first stop, as well as tickets to the Hollywood Bowl for the day's finale. In between, you'll see landmarks in pop culture, experience the majestic Getty Center, and wind along the city's most scenic and historical roads. START: **Burbank.**

❶ ★★ Warner Brothers VIP Tour.
Start the day early in Burbank because that's how the ghost of studio chief Jack Warner would want it. Warner Brothers, the third-oldest movie studio (founded in 1918), took over 110 acres from First National Pictures in 1928 with the payout from betting big on the first "talkie," *The Jazz Singer*. The 2¼-hour tour takes you behind the scenes of the working lot, and with roughly 35 soundstages and outdoor sets, there's a lot of work going on. The hit television show *ER* is shot here, as were *The Dukes of Hazzard*, *The West Wing*, and *Friends*. In fact, the Central Perk coffeehouse set remains intact, and you might have a chance to snap a shot of yourself on the famous couch (Chandler Bing not included). But it's the studio's film history that boggles the mind—*My Fair Lady*, *Rebel Without a Cause*, and *Bonnie and Clyde* were all made here. Standing on the hallowed ground where *Casablanca* was shot, take a moment to imagine Bogie

Take a guided tour of the Warner Brothers lot.

telling Ingrid Bergman, "We'll always have Burbank." Children under 8 are not admitted. Reservations are recommended and can be made online. ⏱ *2–3 hr. 3400 Riverside Dr., Burbank.* ☎ *818/972-8687. www. wbstudiotour.com. Tours $45. Guided tours Mon–Fri, every half-hour 8:30am–4pm (extended hours in spring & summer).*

Coming from Riverside Dr., head left on Olive Ave., continue on Barham Blvd., turn left at Cahuenga Blvd., continue on Highland Ave., and look for a parking structure on your right after you pass Franklin Ave. Park here.

❷ ★ Hollywood and Highland.
After languishing for years as flypaper for runaways and hustlers, Hollywood Boulevard has Times Squared itself in the past decade and is now a polished link to Tinseltown's heyday. The centerpiece of the area's revitalization is the retail and entertainment behemoth at Hollywood and Highland, which includes the grand Kodak Theatre, the first permanent home of the Academy Awards. Explore the multitiered Babylonian-style courtyard, inspired by D. W. Griffith's silent film epic *Intolerance*, and you'll find photo-ready views of the HOLLYWOOD sign perched atop Mount Lee in the distance. ⏱ *30 min. 6801 Hollywood Blvd., at Highland Ave.* ☎ *323/817-0200. www. hollywoodandhighland.com. Mon–Sat 10am–10pm, Sun 10am–7pm.*

You can leave your car in the Hollywood & Highland parking complex; the next stops are walkable.

3 Beard Papa Sweets Café. Grab one exquisitely calibrated cream puff to go. And I do mean go—if you stay, you might not be able to stop eating. *6801 Hollywood Blvd., #153.* ☎ *323/462-6100. $.*

4 ★★ Grauman's Chinese Theatre. "Over the top" would be an understatement. The bronze pagoda roof, garish columns, leering gargoyles, and fiery dragons—for mad impresario Sid Grauman, these were only half the fun. According to the apocryphal story, silent-film star Norma Talmadge accidentally stepped in a patch of wet cement at the theater's opening (the 1927 premiere of Cecil B. DeMille's *The King of Kings*) and the great imprinting tradition was born. A less dramatic version says Grauman got the idea when he observed his chief mason signing his work (look for J.W.K.). Today, the Forecourt of the Stars is cemented in history, crammed with the handprints and footprints of more than 200 movie legends. Perusing them all might leave you with a few questions: Is there a more famous movie theater on the planet? Are Marilyn Monroe's feet really that tiny? Do I have time to catch a matinee? ⏱ *45 min. 6925 Hollywood Blvd.* ☎ *323/464-8111. www.manntheatres.com. Open daily; check website for showtimes.*

5 ★ Walk of Fame. On 18 blocks of pink terrazzo stars, you can find more than 2,000 names—some unforgettable, some already forgotten, and others perhaps less than deserving (sorry, I just don't think Godzilla is much of an actor). Joanne Woodward received the first star in 1960, and Gene Autry received the most, one for each of the five categories: film, television, music, radio, and theater. Immortality doesn't come cheap; the honoree must fork over $25,000 (a "sponsorship fee") to cover installation and maintenance. Be sure to poke your head up every once in a while as you shuffle along, or you could miss other landmarks: the immaculate El Capitan Theatre (6838 Hollywood Blvd.), which premiered *Citizen Kane* in 1941; the Hollywood Roosevelt (7000 Hollywood Blvd.), where the first Academy Awards were held; and another Sid Grauman inspiration, the Egyptian Theatre (6712 Hollywood Blvd.), now home to the American Cinematheque. ⏱ *30 min.; best times are weekday mornings. Hollywood Blvd. from La Brea Ave. to Gower St. & down Vine St. from Yucca St. to Sunset Blvd.*

John Travolta's star on the Walk of Fame.

The gardens at the Getty Center are as impressive as the architecture.

6 Pig'n Whistle. Food options abound at the Hollywood and Highland center, but if you're looking for old-school ambience, duck in here for slightly upscale pub fare. *6714 Hollywood Blvd.* ☎ *323/463-0000. $$.*

Back in your car: From Hollywood and Highland, head east to Vine St., take a right on Vine St., and take another right on Sunset Blvd.

7 ★★ Sunset Boulevard. If you have to choose only one road by which to see the city of Los Angeles, this is the one. Beginning near El Pueblo, the historic core of Downtown, and stretching nearly 25 miles west to the Pacific Ocean, Sunset links working-class ethnic communities (Hispanic, Armenian, Thai), bohemian Silver Lake, historic Hollywood, the always rockin' Sunset Strip, exclusive Beverly Hills and Bel Air, U.C.L.A., and the Pacific Palisades. For an abbreviated tour, start in Hollywood at Sunset and Vine and head west. You can't miss the Cinerama Dome (6360 Sunset Blvd.), which anchors the ArcLight Cinemas complex, where serious cineastes get their fix. When you hit Crescent Heights, you're officially on the

world-famous Sunset Strip. Keep your eyes peeled—the names are going to jump out at you hard and fast: Chateau Marmont (no. 8221), the Standard (no. 8300), the Sunset Tower (no. 8358), the Viper Room (no. 8852), and Whisky a Go Go (no. 8901), to name just a few. By the time you reach the pink palace of the Beverly Hills Hotel (no. 9641), you're loving the lushness of Beverly Hills. Continue on past the gates of Bel Air and the U.C.L.A. campus until you reach Sepulveda Blvd. 🕐 *45 min.*

Head west on Sunset Blvd., take a right at Sepulveda Blvd., and follow the signs for the Getty Center.

8 ★★★ kids Getty Center. Money can't buy happiness, but J. Paul Getty's $1.2 billion bought plenty of world-class art (works by van Gogh, Monet, and Man Ray, among others) and an architectural marvel in which to display it—that makes you a little happy, right? Ascend the acropolis and admire the way Richard Meier ballasts his modern, airy design with textured travertine blocks. But don't forget about the art on the inside. Grab a *GettyGuide* ($5), your own personal digital docent, and go. *See the mini-tour on p 12.*

The Getty Center

Auditorium

Getty Center Dr.

N. Sepulveda Blvd.

405

San Diego Fwy.

8A Arrival Plaza

Restaurant and Cafe

Museum Entrance Hall

Museum Shop

North Pavilion

East Pavilion

8F²

8D

Research Institute

8E

8B

8C

West Pavilion

South Pavilion

A 5-minute **8A tram ride** transports you from the parking area up the hill to the museum and provides the first of many excellent views; for now, just pity those poor saps on the 405 freeway. Head across the courtyard to the terrace of the West Pavilion for the **8B photography collection,** which traces the history of the medium and includes many Man Ray prints, such as the famous *Tears.* Take the elevator two floors to the upper level to **8C paintings** (after 1800). On your right are a couple of Impressionist gems by Claude Monet: *Wheatstacks, Snow Effect, Morning* and *The Portal of Rouen Cathedral in Morning Light.* Screaming at you from the next wall is the

room's rock star, Vincent van Gogh's *Irises,* created in a Saint-Rémy asylum the year before he died. If your creative juices are flowing, make for the **8D sketching gallery** in the upper level of the East Pavilion. Here you can borrow a pencil and a sketch pad to re-create the artwork on display in the studio. Afterward, take a stroll through the delightful and ever-evolving **8E Central Garden.** Then relax at the **8F² Garden Terrace Café** with a coffee or snack and get your fill of scenic wonder. ⏱ *2 hr. 1200 Getty Center Dr.* ☎ *310/440-7300. www.getty.edu. Free admission. Tues–Thurs & Sun 10am–6pm, Fri–Sat 10am–9pm. Closed major holidays. Parking $8.*

Van Gogh's Irises.

Head north on the 405, exit Mulholland Dr., and head east.

⑨ ★★ Mulholland Drive.

Rolling east along the ridge of the Santa Monica Mountains and away from the setting sun, you can watch the canyons pooling with diffuse golden light. It can be hard to keep your eyes on the road, so pull off into one of the many overlooks to take in vistas of the Los Angeles basin to the south and the San Fernando Valley to the north. Repeat as necessary, because an overload of these curves (or worse, tailgating cars) can be as disorienting as watching David Lynch's *Mulholland Drive.* ⏱ 45 min.

From Mulholland Dr., take a right at Cahuenga Blvd., and continue on Highland Ave.

⑩ ★★★ Hollywood Bowl. Fan-

tastic music, a cool summer evening, a lush green hillside, and an arresting venue steeped in entertainment history—a night at the Hollywood Bowl is a consummate Los Angeles experience. The Bowl derives its name not from its famous backdrop of concentric arches, but from the way Mother Nature cups her hands into a 60-acre canyon once known as Daisy Dell. One of the world's largest natural amphitheaters, the Bowl was built in 1922 and holds nearly 18,000 people. The bleachers can be a blast, but if you decide to splurge on box seats, you won't regret it. You can even have a multi-course meal brought right to your box (buy tickets well in advance and order your dinner the day before by 4pm). A diverse schedule—including acts as distinct as the L.A. Philharmonic and Willie Nelson—makes it easy to pick the right night for you. Be sure to come early to check out the Bowl Museum, take a self-guided Bowl Walk, or just relax with a bottle of wine. ⏱ *2–3 hr. 2301 N. Highland Ave.* ☎ *323/850-2000. www.hollywoodbowl.com. Tickets $1–$105. June–Sept.*

⑪ ★ Musso and Frank Grill.

Need a nightcap? The town's oldest restaurant (established in 1919) was once a workday watering hole for writers such as F. Scott Fitzgerald, William Faulkner, Dorothy Parker, and Raymond Chandler, who they say wrote *The Big Sleep* while boozing in a red-leather booth in the back. Plop into a seat at the counter, order one of their mean martinis, and let yourself slowly drift back in time. When you start calling the bartender "doll face," he'll let you know it's time to go. *6667 Hollywood Blvd.* ☎ *323/ 467-7788. $$.*

A stiff drink at the Musso and Frank Grill will do you right.

The Best **in Two Days**

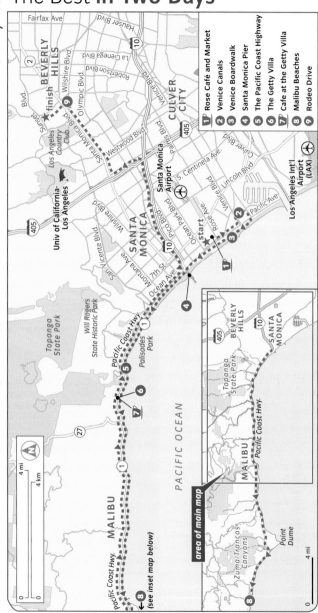

1 Rose Café and Market
2 Venice Canals
3 Venice Boardwalk
4 Santa Monica Pier
5 The Pacific Coast Highway
6 The Getty Villa
7 Cafe at the Getty Villa
8 Malibu Beaches
9 Rodeo Drive

area of main map

PACIFIC OCEAN

MALIBU

Point Dume

Zuma/Trancas Canyons

(see inset map below)

Pacific Coast Hwy.

Topanga State Park

Will Rogers State Historic Park

Palisades Park

Pacific Coast Hwy.

SANTA MONICA

Univ of California–Los Angeles

Los Angeles Country Club

BEVERLY HILLS

CULVER CITY

Santa Monica Airport

Los Angeles Int'l Airport (LAX)

start

finish

Fairfax Ave

Hauser Blvd

Wilshire Blvd

La Cienega Blvd

Robertson Blvd

Olympic Blvd

Santa Monica Blvd

Westwood Blvd

Sunset Blvd

San Vicente Blvd

Montana Ave

Ocean Ave

7th St.

Pico Blvd

Ocean Park Blvd

Rose Ave

Venice Blvd

Lincoln Blvd

Pacific Ave

S. Centinela Ave.

Palms Blvd

Culver Blvd

If you made it through day 1, you've earned a few hours at the beach. Catch the buzz of bustling Venice Boardwalk, then drift up the Pacific Coast Highway past Santa Monica, and splash in the waves of Malibu. Finish up with some hoity-toity shopping on Beverly Hills's Rodeo Drive. START: **Venice.**

1 Rose Café and Market. A Venice institution for nearly 30 years, this lively cafe will jump-start your day with a cup of joe and something fresh from the bakery (as far as selection goes, the earlier the better—the muffins and scones go like, well, hot cakes). *220 Rose Ave.* ☎ *310/399-0711. $.*

Head west on Rose Ave., go left at Speedway, and look for parking lots along Venice Blvd.

2 ★ Venice Canals. The image of these canals, like the HOLLYWOOD sign, is a Los Angeles icon born of a busted real-estate venture. In the early 1900s, entrepreneur Abbot Kinney dreamt up "Venice of America," 16 miles of canals connecting piers, theaters, restaurants, and hotels; he even imported a couple dozen gondoliers from Italy. Cars or gondolas: Guess what won out in the long run? Today only a handful of canals and bridges remain, and they form a quaint residential nook. Cute, decades-old bungalows and

modernist McMansions flank the canals, which are dotted with ducks and small boats. A peaceful setting for a morning stroll. ⏱ *30 min. Venice Blvd. (btwn Pacific & Ocean aves.), Venice. Start at the Grand Canal & follow the bridges.*

3 ★★★ Venice Boardwalk. When I say it's a "complete freak show," I mean that lovingly. L.A. has a rich history of people who require a lot of attention, and the Venice Boardwalk is where exhibitionists come to out-exhibit each other: messiahs in Reeboks, amateur acrobats, jewelry-bedecked pit bulls, and a ubiquitous Rollerblading, electric guitar–playing dude who seems to be everywhere at once. Join a drum circle, get a henna tattoo, join a political movement you've never heard of, help the skate rats with their *Jackass* audition, or even join the grunts of the Muscle Beachheads. Or take a front-row seat at the **Sidewalk Café** (1401 Ocean Front Walk) and watch it all through a pair of cheap sunglasses that you'll lose by the end of your

Houses run alongside the canals in Venice Beach.

trip. 🕐 *1–2 hr. Ocean Front Walk (btwn Venice Blvd. & Rose Ave.), Venice.*

Take Pacific Ave. north, continue on Ocean Ave., and take a left at Colorado Ave.

4 ★ Santa Monica Pier. This century-old slice of Americana is considered the end of the line of the legendary Route 66. If you're catching a Coney Island vibe, that might be because it was designed by amusement-park pioneer Charles Looff, the man who carved the first wooden carousel at Coney Island. Today the Pier's gorgeous Looff Hippodrome Carousel building is a National Historic Landmark (and not just for its plum roles in film and television, such as in the opening credits of *Three's Company*). For a great panorama of the entire Santa Monica Bay, head to the far end of the pier or, even better, take a spin on the world's first solar-powered Ferris wheel, which sends you nine stories above the water. 🕐 *30 min. Colorado Ave. at Ocean Ave., Santa Monica.* ☎ *310/458-8900. www.santamonicapier.org.*

From the pier, turn right (south) on Ocean Ave., then turn right on the CA-1/PCH ramp.

The entrance to the Santa Monica Pier.

Greek, Roman, and Etruscan artifacts are on display at the Getty Villa.

Go north on the Pacific Coast Hwy. (PCH).

5 ★ The Pacific Coast Highway. If you haven't dropped the top of your convertible, now might be a good time. The PCH hugs the dramatic California coastline all the way to the San Francisco Bay area and beyond. But we don't need to go that far to get the picture. The ocean shimmers to the west, the warm wind whips your hair, and you finally find a song you dig on the radio—it's little moments like this that keep Angelenos addicted to their cars. 🕐 *30 min. Pacific Coast Hwy.*

6 ★★ The Getty Villa. Little (but older) sibling of the Getty Center, the Getty Villa is entirely dedicated to ancient Greek, Roman, and Etruscan art. In 1974, when J. Paul Getty's art collection overran his Malibu ranch home (don't you hate it when that happens?), he had a museum built next door and modeled it after the Roman Villa dei Papiri in Herculaneum. The collection grew and, in 1997, moved into bigger digs: the celebrated Getty Center a few miles away in Brentwood. Reopened in 2006 after a 9-year, $275-million makeover, the Villa displays roughly 1,200 artifacts from 6500 B.C. to A.D. 600 (from a total collection of 44,000 items). Fittingly, you enter the lavish grounds from an elevated walkway, as if stumbling across an archaeological dig. Wander the sun-drenched formal gardens (even the smelly one, the Herb Garden, which grows herbs popular with the ancient Romans), and soak in the magnificent Pacific views. Admission is limited to around 1,200 people a day, so reservations are a must. The

Designer stores line famed Rodeo Drive.

museum remains a hot ticket, despite being dogged by charges from the Greek and Italian governments that some artifacts were acquired illegally. ⏱ *1 hr. 17985 Pacific Coast Hwy., Malibu.* ☎ *310/ 440-7300. www.getty.edu. Thurs– Mon 10am–5pm. Reservations strongly recommended. Free admission. Parking $8.*

7 Cafe at the Getty Villa. Mediterranean-inspired lunch fare is simple, but it's made tastier by an outdoor patio with a killer view. *Thurs–Mon 11am–4:30pm. $.*

Head west along the PCH.

8 ★★★ Malibu Beaches. Malibu has several great beach options depending on what floats your boat. The most popular and most accessible choice is **Zuma Beach,** a wide, family-friendly stretch with plenty of activities, snack shacks, and restrooms. Just south is my favorite beach, **Point Dume,** which lacks the Zuma amenities, but also its crowds. The **Robert H. Meyer Memorial State Beach** is a few miles north and is actually three minibeaches: **El Matador, La Piedra,** and **El Pescador.** Each of these rocky coves has little parking and no facilities, and can only be reached by trails and tricky stairways. Set against the Malibu cliffs, these beaches are both cozy and rugged. You might have a

hard time choosing between splashing in the waves, climbing the rocks, or exploring the tide pools. ⏱ *2 hr. Point Dume: 7103 Westward Rd., Malibu.* ☎ *310/457-9701. Zuma Beach: 30000 Pacific Coast Hwy., Malibu.* ☎ *310/457-9701. Robert H. Meyer Memorial State Beach: 33000 Pacific Coast Hwy., Malibu.* ☎ *818/ 880-0350. Daily 7am–10pm.*

Head east on the PCH, go east on I-10, go north on I-405, exit on Santa Monica Blvd., and head east. Bear right at Wilshire Blvd.

9 ★★ Rodeo Drive. If the beach doesn't have the cure for what ails you, perhaps some serious retail therapy is in order. In the "Golden Triangle" of Beverly Hills (Santa Monica Blvd., Wilshire Blvd., and Crescent Dr.), the doctor is in, though his rates are sky-high. No street says "beautiful-things-I-can't-afford" quite like fabled Rodeo Drive. Gucci, Versace, Cartier, and Tiffany—all the biggest names in fashion and jewelry design are here. The most popular spot for "look, I was there" snapshots is the "Spanish Steps" that descend from the pedestrian-only cobblestone path, Via Rodeo, to Wilshire Boulevard. Directly across the street stands the Beverly Wilshire, where the *Pretty Woman* was swept off her feet. ⏱ *30 min. 200–500 Rodeo Dr. (at Wilshire Blvd.), Beverly Hills. Most shops are open Mon–Sat 10am–6pm, Sun noon–5pm. Public parking $2 per hour.*

The Best **in Three Days**

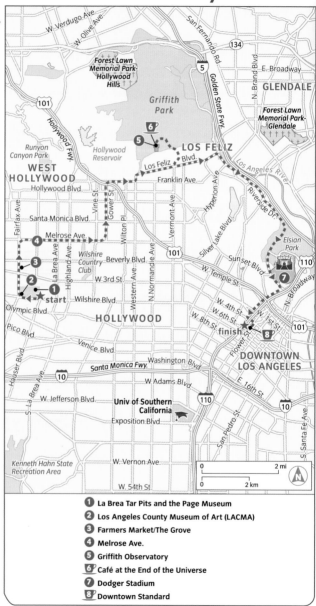

1 La Brea Tar Pits and the Page Museum

2 Los Angeles County Museum of Art (LACMA)

3 Farmers Market/The Grove

4 Melrose Ave.

5 Griffith Observatory

6 Café at the End of the Universe

7 Dodger Stadium

8 Downtown Standard

After 2 jam-packed days, it's time to stop and smell the hydrogen sulfide (bubbling up from the La Brea Tar Pits). Then you'll sample the city's most extensive collection of art at LACMA, have lunch at the Farmers Market, and scope out the freshly renovated Griffith Observatory. Cap your 3 days with a blast Downtown at Dodger Stadium. START: **Mid-Wilshire area.**

① ★ kids The La Brea Tar Pits and the Page Museum. Ready for some stinky pools of tar? Well, actually, it's asphalt, and it's been seeping out of the ground here on 23 acres of Hancock Park for the last 40,000 years. In the last Ice Age, animals roaming the Los Angeles Basin would sometimes get trapped by the sticky pools and sucked into the ground where the asphalt would eventually fossilize the remains. Today the collection at the Page Museum holds around a million bones from more than 200 species of invertebrates, including the long extinct Columbian mammoth and saber-toothed cat. The first excavations occurred in 1906, and the search for fossils continues to this day. If you visit during July and August, there's a good chance you can observe scientists at work on Pit 91. The gift shop has great toys for budding paleontologists. ⏱ *1 hr. 5801 Wilshire Blvd.* ☎ *323/934-7243.*

www.tarpits.org. Mon–Fri 9:30am–5pm, Sat–Sun 10am–5pm. $7 adults, $4.50 seniors & students, $2 kids 5–12, free for kids under 5.

② ★★★ kids Los Angeles County Museum of Art (LACMA). The LACMA may not boast the stunning architecture of the Getty Center or its easy-flow layout, but it does offer more art than you could possibly hope to see in 1 day. Heck, you can run out of breath just attempting to list the collections: American (John Singer Sargent, Mary Cassatt), Latin American (Diego Riviera), European, Islamic, Japanese (with its own Asian–meets–*The Jetsons* building), modern (Picasso, Chagall, Matisse, Kandinsky), photography (Weston, Evans, Arbus), and several more. One piece of particular interest (because you've done the legwork) is David Hockney's exuberant *Mulholland Drive, The Road to the Studio.* The offerings are too

A woolly mammoth rises from the tar at the La Brea Tar Pits.

The Grove, an outdoor shopping mall.

diverse to simply start wandering—grab a guide and make a game plan. ⏱ *1–2 hr. 5905 Wilshire Blvd.* ☎ *323/857-6000. www.lacma.org. Mon–Tues & Thurs noon–8pm, Fri noon–9pm, Sat–Sun 11am–8pm.*

From LACMA, head west on Wilshire Blvd. and take a right on Fairfax Ave.

③ ★ kids Farmers Market/ The Grove. During the Great Depression, on a dirt parking lot at the corner of Third Street and Fairfax Avenue, local farmers began selling their fresh produce out of the backs of their trucks. Folks poured in and, before long, a maze of wooden stalls sprung up, with butcher shops, bakeries, and restaurants adding to the mix. Surprisingly, the market today manages to retain its folksy charms (as well as its clock tower from 1941). Sure, there are plenty of tourists, but there are even more locals—power players on a lunch break, Russian retirees playing chess, mommies pushing strollers, and solitary artsy types contemplating big ideas. Favorite eateries include the Gumbo Pot for (you guessed it) Cajun-style gumbo, Loteria! Grill for authentic Mexican food, and Kokomo Café for BLTs and other diner staples. Less-than-fun fact: James Dean is said to have picked up breakfast at the Farmers Market the morning of his fatal road trip. Never fear—you can ride the Disney-like trolley a few hundred feet to your next stop, The Grove, an elaborate outdoor mall which has been hugely popular since its debut in 2002. With its faux-European architecture and water fountain that mesmerizes kids,

For unbeatable views of the city, head to the Griffith Observatory.

Treat yourself to America's favorite pastime with an outing to Dodger Stadium. See p 22.

the experience is equal parts fab and pre-fab. ⏱ *1–2 hr. Farmers Market: 6333 W. Third St. www.farmersmarket la.com.* ☎ *323/933-9211. Mon–Fri 9am–9pm, Sat 9am–8pm, Sun 10am–7pm. The Grove: 189 The Grove Dr.* ☎ *323/900-8080. www.thegrovela. com. Mon–Thurs 10am–9pm, Fri–Sat 10am–10pm, Sun 11am–8pm.*

Exit on Fairfax Ave. and head north; take a right on Melrose Ave.

④ Melrose Avenue. In dire need of vintage tees, tattoos, or tips on how to chop/sculpt/dye your hair? The blocks between Fairfax and La Brea avenues make a fascinating cruise of scruffy shops and restaurants.

Head east on Melrose Ave., then take a left on Gower St., a right on Franklin Ave., a left on Western Ave., and a left on Vermont Ave. Follow the signs to the observatory.

⑤ ★★★ kids Griffith Observatory. Like so many iconic beauties in Los Angeles, the Griffith Observatory has had a teensy amount of work done—about 4 years' and $93 million's worth. As of the fall of 2006, she is ready for her close-up.

Architectural details have been spit-shined to their original 1930s grandeur; a 40,000-square-foot expansion has added exhibits, a classroom, theater, and cafe; and the Samuel Oschin Planetarium has undergone a massive overhaul (sorry, no more Pink Floyd laser shows). Due to the overwhelming number of new visitors, it's necessary to make a timed-entry and shuttle reservation (☎ 888/695-0888). Be aware, however, that a timed-entry reservation does not include admission to the planetarium show. Those tickets are available at the observatory only and often sell out. Before you step inside, circle the grounds and admire the building's beautiful Art Deco architecture and the stellar views of the city stretched out below. ⏱ *1–2 hr. 2800 E. Observatory Rd.* ☎ *213/473-0800. www.griffithobservatory.org. Tues–Fri noon–10pm, Sat–Sun 10am–10pm.*

⑥ Café at the End of the Universe. The views may trump the menu, but you can't go wrong snacking it up on this sunny terrace catered by Wolfgang Puck. *In the Griffith Observatory. $.*

Sipping a cocktail at the Downtown Standard is an oh-so-hip way to end your day.

Head east on Los Feliz Blvd., then south on Riverside Dr., and bear right on Stadium Way.

7 ★★ kids **Dodger Stadium.** Don't underestimate the simple pleasure of taking in a baseball game in southern California on a spring or summer evening. Since 1962 Angelenos have rooted on the Dodgers at classic Dodger Stadium, the fifth-oldest stadium in the league. Kick back with a Dodger Dog in cushy box seats, or whoop it up with the die-hards in the bleachers. If it's not baseball season, check out what's scheduled at the Walt Disney Concert Hall (p 130). *1000 Elysian Park Ave.* ☎ *866-DODGERS.*

www.dodgers.com. Most night games 7:10pm; most day games 1:10pm. Check schedule for specific dates & times. Tickets $10–$225.

Head south on I-110, exit Fourth St.; turn right on Flower St.

8 ★★ **Standard Downtown.** This groovy nightspot single-handedly launched the city's rooftop bar trend. A swimming pool, skyscraper views, and space-pod waterbeds—your head is spinning before you can order your first cocktail. *550 S. Flower St., at Sixth St.* ☎ *213/892-8080. www.standardhotel.com. $.* ●

L.A. for **Movie Buffs**

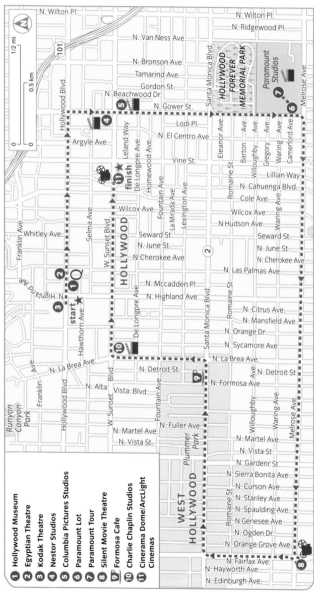

1. Hollywood Museum
2. Egyptian Theatre
3. Kodak Theatre
4. Nestor Studios
5. Columbia Pictures Studios
6. Paramount Lot
7. Paramount Tour
8. Silent Movie Theatre
9. Formosa Cafe
10. Charlie Chaplin Studios
11. Cinerama Dome/ArcLight Cinemas

Previous page: Celebrity impersonators line the Hollywood Walk of Fame.

Have you done your homework by watching hundreds and hundreds of Hollywood films? Good, then let's go find out where they came from. Aaaand action! START: **Park in the Hollywood and Highland complex and walk to the first three stops.**

❶ ★ Hollywood Museum.

Don't make the mistake of lumping this in with tourist traps like the Hollywood Wax or Ripley's Believe It or Not! museums. This museum—occupying the historic Max Factor building, restored to its full Art Deco loveliness—traces the history of film with 5,000 displays of rare Hollywood memorabilia, such as Hannibal Lecter's cell block, Indiana Jones's whip, Rita Hayworth's makeup case, Cary Grant's Rolls-Royce, and the earliest film cameras. ⏱ *1 hr. 1660 N. Highland Ave., at Hollywood Blvd.* ☎ *323/464-7776. www.thehollywood museum.com. Thurs–Sun 10am–5pm. $15 adults, $12 seniors & children under 12. Parking $2 w/validation.*

The courtyard of Sid Grauman's famed Egyptian Theatre.

❷ ★ Egyptian Theatre.

In 1922, as the hunt closed in on King Tut's tomb, Sid Grauman unveiled the Egyptian Theatre, the first of his spectacular, themed movie palaces. Reopened in 1998 following a multi-million-dollar restoration, the theater is now the home of the nonprofit American Cinematheque, which caters to serious film enthusiasts. It offers fresh, 70mm prints of classics *(Lawrence of Arabia, The Sound of Music);* programs of national cinema (Classic Italian, Russian Fantastik, and British New Wave); director retrospectives (Douglas Sirk, Orson Welles); and in-person tributes to actors and filmmakers (George Clooney, Quentin Tarantino). If nothing else, catch one of the daily screenings of *Forever Hollywood,* an hour-long look at a century of cinema. ⏱ *1 hr. 6712 Hollywood Blvd.* ☎ *323/466-FILM.*

www.egyptiantheatre.com. Forever Hollywood $7 adults, $5 seniors & students.

❸ ★ Kodak Theatre.

If you're a person who hosts an Oscar® party every year at home with your own printed ballots, a 30-minute walking tour of the Kodak Theatre will tickle your fancy. You'll see the grand entrance (you'll have to imagine the red carpet), a few Oscar® statuettes, the 3,300-seat auditorium inspired by a European opera house, and the backstage VIP area. The Kodak is also home to the *American Idol* finals. ⏱ *30 min. 6801 Hollywood Blvd., at Highland Ave.* ☎ *323/308-6300. www. kodaktheatre.com. Jun–Aug Mon–Sun 10:30am–4pm;*

An Oscar® statue outside the Kodak Theatre.

The Kodak Theatre on its biggest night of the year.

Sept–May Mon–Sun 10:30am–2:30pm. $15 adults, $10 seniors & children 3 & up, free for children under 3.

Head east on Hollywood Blvd., then south on Gower St.

4 Nestor Studios. In an old tavern on the northwest corner of Sunset and Gower, the Nestor Company launched the first film studio in Hollywood in 1911. Using natural California sunshine and a small wooden stage, several one-reelers were shot each week: one Western, one drama, one comedy. Other film pioneers soon followed, including Cecil B. DeMille, Jesse Lasky, and D. W. Griffith. In 1912 Nestor merged with Carl Laemmle's Universal Film Company. The original building was razed in 1936 to make room for the CBS Columbia Square radio studio, which can be seen today. 🕐 *10 min. Sunset Blvd. & Gower St., northwest corner.*

5 Columbia Pictures Studios. On the southeast corner of the same intersection sit the Sunset-Gower studios, formerly the home of Columbia Pictures Studios (1921–72), which produced countless gems such as *It Happened One Night, From Here to Eternity, Dr. Strangelove,* and *Funny Girl.* 🕐 *10 min. 1438 N. Gower St.*

Head south on Gower St. to Melrose Ave.

6 Paramount Lot. Paramount Studios traces its origins to a rented horse barn near Sunset and Vine in 1913. Thirteen years later, it moved to its current location and never left, unlike the rest of the major studios in Hollywood. From Melrose Avenue you can see the famous "Bronson Gate," the arched gateway you may remember Gloria Swanson driving through in *Sunset Boulevard.* The back lot eventually gobbled up neighboring R.K.O. Pictures, and the distinctive globe is still visible in the southwest corner. 🕐 *10 min. 5555 Melrose Ave.* ☎ *323/956-1777. www.paramount.com.*

7 ★ Paramount Tour. For a closer look at the massive studio, book tickets in advance for a 2-hour walking tour, which trots you through the "living history" of its film and television soundstages. This is where the stars punch the clock, so keep your eyes peeled for sightings (but no snapshots). Don't get so caught up gawking that you forget whose footsteps you're walking in: Rudolph Valentino, Mary Pickford, W. C. Fields, Alfred Hitchcock, the Marx Brothers, Bob Hope, and many more. 🕐 *2 hr. 5555 Melrose Ave.* ☎ *323/956-1777. www.paramount.com. Mon–Fri 10am–2pm. Tours $35. Children under 12 not admitted.*

Head west on Melrose Ave., and then south on Fairfax Ave.

⑧ Silent Movie Theatre. This little theater, a 200-seater, screens silent films with live music accompaniment, often preceded by silent shorts, cartoons, and serials. The theater is sometimes rented out for private events, so the schedule can be erratic; the new owners are even talking about booking talkies. But with a little luck, you can catch a Keaton comedy, or a program packing as much vampy fun as last summer's Screen Sirens (films with Theda Bara, Louise Brooks, and Gloria Swanson). 🕐 *1½ hr. 611 N. Fairfax Ave.* ☎ *323/655-2520. www.silentmovietheatre.com. Tickets $10. Check website for schedule.*

Head north on Fairfax Ave., and then east on Santa Monica Blvd.

⑨ ★★ Formosa Cafe. The shiny, strip-mall surroundings may throw you, but trust me: This is a vintage Hollywood watering hole. Formosa Cafe has always attracted celebrity lunch-timers and late-nighters. Marilyn Monroe and Clark Gable shared a red-leather booth while taking a break from shooting *The Misfits.* Bogie, Sinatra, Brando, and, in recent years, Bono, have all sidled up to this bar. The walls display hundreds of signed photos of its celebrity fans. The food is nothing special, but the atmosphere you can eat with a spoon. *7156 Santa Monica Blvd., at Formosa Ave.* ☎ *323/850-9050. $.*

Take Santa Monica Blvd. east to La Brea Ave., and then head north.

⑩ Charlie Chaplin Studios. In 1917, on acres of orange groves at Sunset and La Brea, Charlie Chaplin built himself a studio, a row of English-style cottages (perhaps trying to create a happy and sunny version of his childhood). Chaplin shot many of his classics here, such as *The Gold Rush, City Lights,* and *Modern Times.* Today Jim Henson Productions occupies the building, which features a statue of Kermit the Frog donning The Little Tramp's familiar bowler hat, cane, and tails. 🕐 *10 min. 1416 N. La Brea Ave.*

Go north on La Brea Ave., and then east on Sunset Blvd.

⑪ ★ Cinerama Dome/ArcLight Cinemas. Built in 1963 to showcase the widescreen format, the landmark Cinerama Dome now belongs to the state-of-the-art ArcLight Complex of 14 theaters. While the Dome is the coolest with its curving, immersive screen, all of the theaters feature sumptuous assigned seating, immaculate sound, and detail-oriented service. 🕐 *1½–2 hr. 6160 W. Sunset Blvd. (btwn Vine St. & Ivar Ave.).* ☎ *323/ 464-1478. www.arclightcinemas. com. Tickets $7.75–$14. Parking $2 for 4 hr. w/validation.*

Inside the Cinerama Dome at the ArcLight Cinemas.

L.A. for **Kids**

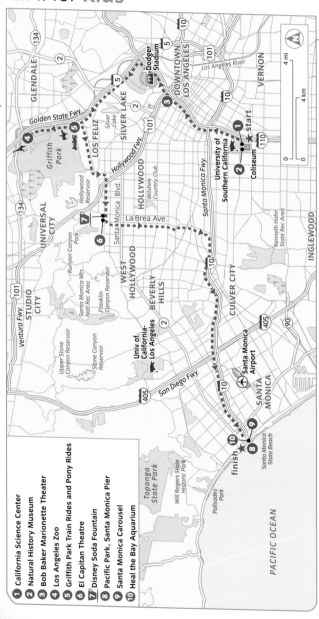

1 California Science Center
2 Natural History Museum
3 Bob Baker Marionette Theater
4 Los Angeles Zoo
5 Griffith Park Train Rides and Pony Rides
6 El Capitan Theatre
7 Disney Soda Fountain
8 Pacific Park, Santa Monica Pier
9 Santa Monica Carousel
10 Heal the Bay Aquarium

Let's be honest: Kids' moods can be as unpredictable as Los Angeles traffic. By no means do I recommend trying to hit *every* stop on this list. Let your kid be the guide. START: **700 State Dr.**

1 ★★ California Science Center. This interactive museum about science and technology never fails to dazzle kids of all ages. Watch an IMAX movie in 3-D on L.A.'s biggest screen (seven stories high!), or investigate exhibits like *Goose Bumps! The Science of Fear*. Take a spin on a high-wire bicycle, or strap into the Millennium Falcon flight simulator. Tess, a 50-foot woman with a see-through body, teaches kids about homeostasis, how the body keeps its system in balance (don't worry, it's perfectly fine if you learn something, too). There are also hands-on areas for younger kids. Check the website for current exhibits and IMAX movies. 🕐 *1–2 hr. 700 State Dr.* ☎ *323/724-3623. Daily 10am–5pm. Free admission. IMAX $5.75–$8. Parking $6.*

2 Natural History Museum. Opened in 1913, this museum is the largest of its kind in the western United States. A scrapbook documenting the history of Mother Earth and her inhabitants, the museum holds 33 million specimens and artifacts, including the Megamouth, the world's rarest shark (only 17 have ever been discovered). But it's

Tess, the 50-foot-tall model at the California Science Center.

the dinosaurs that are the real rock stars among the rocks and fossils; the T. rex skull on display is considered one of the finest anywhere. At the Discovery Center, kids can dirty their hands on their own dig. 🕐 *1 hr. 900 Exposition Blvd., Exposition Park.* ☎ *213/763-DINO. www.nhm.org. $9 adults; $6.50 seniors, students & children 13–17; $2 children 5–12; free for kids under 5. Free for everyone 1st Tues of month. Mon–Fri 9:30am–5pm, Sat–Sun 10am–5pm.*

Take 110 north, exit Third St., and go west. Go right at Lucas St.; the theater is under the bridge.

3 Bob Baker Marionette Theater. With all the high-tech wizardry out there competing for kids' attention, sometimes it's nice to remember the good, old-fashioned fun of watching wooden puppets spring to life with string. Founded in 1963 by puppeteer pioneer Bob Baker, this children's theater company is the oldest in Los Angeles. You'll have to forgive its less-than-pristine exterior; this labor of love is the real deal. Handmade puppets are for sale. 🕐 *1 hr. 1345 W. First St.* ☎ *213/250-9995. www.bobbakermarionettes.com. Shows Tues–Fri 10:30am, Sat–Sun 2:30pm. $15 adults & children, free for kids under 3. Reservations required.*

Take 110 north toward Pasadena, go north on I-5, take 134 east toward Pasadena, and then exit Zoo Dr.

4 ★ Los Angeles Zoo. This zoo occupies 113 hilly acres of prime Griffith Park and is home to over 1,000 animals from 250 species, including the world's rarest bird of prey, the California Condor. Recent additions are the Campo Gorilla

Bob Baker has worked with many Holly-wood legends, including Elvis Presley, The Three Stooges, and Judy Garland (pictured here). See p 29.

Reserve and the Golden Monkey exhibit. Other favorites include the Sea Lion Cliffs, the Chimpanzees of the Mahale Mountains, and the Mandrills Exhibit of the world's biggest and most brightly colored baboons. Just inside the zoo's entrance is the Winnick Family Children's Zoo, where kids can visit the baby animal nursery or make friends with the goats and pot-bellied pigs in the petting zoo. Kids will also want to board the "L.A. Zoo Choo Choo," a colorful little train that stops near the World of Birds. ⏱ 2 hr. 5333 Zoo Dr., Griffith Park. ☎ 323/644-4200. www.lazoo.org. $10 adults, $7 seniors, $5 children 2–12, free for kids under 2. Daily 10am–5pm (July 1–Labor Day till 6pm).

⑤ Griffith Park Train Rides and Pony Rides. This minitrain has chugged through Griffith Park since 1948. It's a mile-long ride through a meadow and an old Western town, and past ponies. When you hear cries for pony rides, don't despair: Little buckaroos and buckarettes can safely ride ponies around a small track. ⏱ 1 hr. 4400 Crystal Springs Dr. (near Los Feliz Blvd. & Riverside Dr.), Griffith Park. ☎ 323/664-6903 (for train rides) or 323/664-3266 (for pony rides). Mon–Fri 10am–4:30pm, Sat–Sun 10am–5pm.

Take Los Feliz Blvd. west, go south on Western Ave., and then head west on Hollywood Blvd.

⑥ El Capitan Theatre. This is *the* spot to catch the latest summer blockbuster from Disney/Pixar. Debuting in 1926 as "Hollywood's First Home of Spoken Drama," the theater has been fully restored to its original grandeur by the Walt Disney Company. El Capitan is one of three themed theaters—along with the Chinese and the Egyptian—from the team of Charles Toberman and Sid Grauman. It boasts a Spanish Colonial facade; a lively, East Indian–influenced interior; and a 2,500-pipe organ from the 1920s called the "Mighty Wurlitzer." Get there early for the preshow song-and-dance numbers by costumed characters. ⏱ 2 hr. 6838 Hollywood Blvd. ☎ 800/347-6396. $13 adults, $10 for children & seniors. $2 discount on adult tickets only at matinees.

⑦ Disney Soda Fountain. Your kids are going to beg you for a milk-shake or a movie-themed sundae at the old-fashioned ice cream parlor next door to El Capitan Theatre. 6834 Hollywood Blvd. ☎ 323/939-9024. $.

Head west on Hollywood Blvd., go south on La Brea Ave., and then head west on I-10; Exit Fourth/Fifth St., go north on Fifth St. to Colorado Ave., and then take a left.

⑧ Pacific Park, Santa Monica Pier. It might not be Disneyland, but, hey, it's on the water and does a good job hearkening back to the turn-of-the-century amusement piers of yesteryear. The Ferris wheel is the high-point, literally and figuratively. ⏱ 1 hr. On the Santa Monica Pier. ☎ 310/260-8744. www.pacpark.com. Summer season: Sun–Thurs 11am–11pm, Fri–Sat 11am–12:30am. All other seasons: Mon–Fri noon–midnight, Sat 11am–midnight, Sun 11am–9pm. Free admission; cost varies per ride.

Universal Studios Hollywood

Although this high-tech theme park may not have the same magical allure as Disneyland, it is close to Hollywood, and it also packs an entertaining, if sanitized, hour-long tour of its moviemaking facilities. In 1915, Carl Laemmle bought 230 acres of farmland just north of Hollywood and built the world's largest motion picture production facility, Universal City Studios (eventually expanding to 420 acres). In the early years, the studio figured the burgeoning film industry needed all the publicity it could get and happily opened its doors to spectators; today the tradition continues (albeit at a much higher price). Popular thrill rides and attractions include the *Revenge of the Mummy* roller coaster, the *Backdraft* simulated warehouse fire, and, my favorite for a hot summer day, the water-soaked *Jurassic Park* river ride. Look for the brand-new *The Simpsons* virtual-reality ride in the summer of 2008. Lines can get long; consider splurging on a "Front of the Line" pass ($109), which eliminates the wait for any ride, or a VIP pass ($199), which combines the "Front of the Line" pass with a private studio tour. Multiday discounts are available online. *100 Universal City Plaza (off the 101 Hollywood Fwy.).* ☎ *818/662-3801. www.universal studioshollywood.com. $61 adults, $51 children under 48 in. tall, free for kids under 3. Call for hours.*

⑨ Santa Monica Carousel.
Built by Charles Looff in 1916, the Looff Hippodrome Carousel building is a National Historic Landmark. The carousel is a spinning spectacle of lights, hand-carved ponies, and brightly colored chariots. The original 1909 merry-go-round was replaced by a "new" one built in 1922. ⏲ *20 min. On the Santa Monica Pier.*

⑩ Heal the Bay Aquarium.
This small, interactive aquarium has three touch tanks where kids can handle (ever so gently) 30 different species common to the Californian shores, such as sea stars, crabs, and sea urchins. Other animals are in observation-only tanks: the two-spotted octopus, the moray eel, California spiny lobster, and flower-like anemones. Don't miss the tank of horn sharks and swell sharks; it's liveliest at feeding time (3:30pm) during the popular Shark Sundays.

⏲ *30 min. 1600 Ocean Front Walk, Santa Monica.* ☎ *310/393-6149. www.healthebay.org. Fall & winter: Tues–Fri 2–5pm, Sat–Sun 12:30–5pm; spring & summer: Tues–Fri 2–6pm, Sat–Sun 12:30–6pm. $2 adults, free for children under 13 when accompanied by an adult.*

Enjoy the view of the beach from the Ferris wheel at Pacific Park.

32

L.A. for **Shopaholics**

The Best Special-Interest Tours

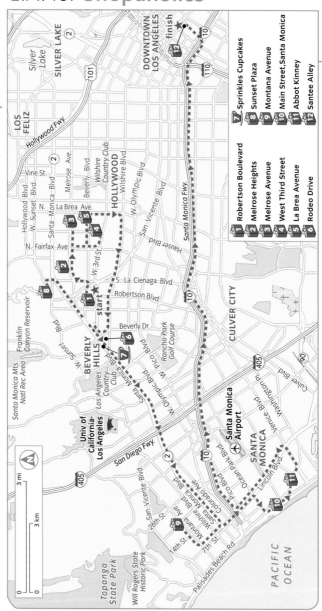

1 Robertson Boulevard
2 Melrose Heights
3 Melrose Avenue
4 West Third Street
5 La Brea Avenue
6 Rodeo Drive
7 Sprinkles Cupcakes
8 Sunset Plaza
9 Montana Avenue
10 Main Street, Santa Monica
11 Abbot Kinney
12 Santee Alley

If you've conquered the Grove, the Beverly Center, and Third Street Promenade, and the serious shopper in you still needs more, try the following shopping areas on for size. Beware: A lot of shopping is listed here, probably more than you (or your wallet) can take in an afternoon. START: **Beverly Hills.**

❶ ★ Robertson Boulevard. Strolling these über-trendy shops, you can sometimes find yourself in the middle of a flashbulb-popping frenzy: Is it the power-broker pow-wow over at the Ivy? Or is Paris Hilton doing an in-store promo at Kitson? Robertson specializes in chic boutiques for chicks: Curve, Vionnet, Nanette Lepore, Lisa Kline, Kate Spade, Madison, Agnes B., and Diavolina. Dudes can make do with John Varvatos, Ted Baker, Lisa Kline for Men, and Camper Shoes—or they can people-watch from a table at the Newsroom Café. *Robertson Blvd. (btwn Beverly Blvd. & Burton Way).*

Head east on Beverly Blvd. to La Cienega Blvd., and then head north to Melrose Ave.

❷ ★ Melrose Heights. This is the spiffier part of Melrose, west of Fairfax, that competes with the high-end designers on Robertson. The area is anchored by the legendary Fred Segal, a must-stop for shopping, but big names have been popping up in recent years, especially along Melrose Place: Marc Jacobs, Diane von Furstenberg, Oscar de la Renta, Carolina Herrera, Marni, and Chloe. There's more fun fashion from Forna-rina, Cynthia Rowley, Paul Smith, and the splashy Betsey Johnson. Divas can inspect Cameron Silver's Decades for vintage couture, or Agent Provocateur for something even slinkier. Also, sniff out Santa Maria Novella, a darling Florentine perfumery. *Melrose Ave. (from La Cienega Blvd. to Fairfax Ave.) & Melrose Place.*

❸ Melrose Avenue. This is the punky kid brother of Melrose Heights, with the same name but a much different attitude. Grab second-hand threads from Aardvark's or Wasteland, and then indulge your inner child with Golden Apple Comics. And instead of a tattoo, how about a frozen yogurt at Pinkberry's? *Melrose Ave. (from Fairfax Ave. to La Brea Ave.).*

Head south on Fairfax Ave. to W. Third St.

❹ ★★ West Third Street. An alternative to the antiseptic experience of the malls (the Beverly Center and the Grove) that bookend it, West Third Street offers a refreshing stretch of independently owned (and independently minded) boutiques. Smart, stylish, eccentric—these shops specialize in the "I had no idea I needed that" experience: cutting-edge fashion at Aero & Co., Scout, Filly, Noodle Stories, Satine, and South Willard; choice vintage wear at Polka Dots & Moonbeams; killer shoes at Sigerson Morrison; mod travel gear at Flight 001; design-heavy gifts at O.K., Zipper, and Plastica; and

Kitson, on Robertson Boulevard, attracts the fabulous and the flashbulbs that follow them.

kiddie coolness at Pipsqueak and Puppies & Babies. *W. Third St. (btwn La Cienega Blvd. & Fairfax Ave.).*

Go north on Fairfax Ave., and then east on Beverly Blvd. to La Brea Ave.

⑤ La Brea Avenue. This is known more as a major north-south thoroughfare than a can't-miss shopping pocket, but there are some great shops you might be zooming by. American Rag Cie has an amazing array of designer wear and quality vintage duds and has tons of premium jeans at their World Denim Bar. For more clothes, try the rock-'n'-rollin' J. Ransom, the ultra-feminine Iconology, or the secondhand selection at Jet Rag. Sneaker freaks love Undefeated, and home decor hunters hit Liz's Antique Hardware, Homework, and Maison Midi. *La Brea Ave. (btwn Wilshire & Beverly blvds.).*

Head south on La Brea Ave., and then go west on Wilshire Blvd.

⑥ ★★ Rodeo Drive. Running through the "Golden Triangle" of Beverly Hills (Santa Monica Blvd., Wilshire Blvd., and Canon Dr.) is

Versace is one of the many high-end stores on famed Rodeo Drive.

world-famous Rodeo Drive. All the top designers vie for your eye: Prada, Chanel, Bulgari, Gucci, Hermès, Louis Vuitton, Michael Kors, Versace, Ralph Lauren, Dolce & Gabbana, Badgley Mischka. And here's an unexpected name: Frank Lloyd Wright. He designed the Anderton Court building at 322 N. Rodeo Dr., one of his only commercial properties. Veering off Rodeo Drive you'll find Lily et Cie, high-end vintage glam; Pixie Town, for kids with means; Taschen, magnificent books on architecture and photography; Edelweiss Chocolates, a Beverly Hills sugar institution for 65 years; and Jimmy Choo shoes. *Rodeo Dr. (btwn Santa Monica Blvd., Wilshire Blvd. & Canon Dr.).*

⑦ Sprinkles Cupcakes. This cute cupcakery with a cult following has lines spilling out onto the sidewalk and some of the most delectable cupcakes you'll ever stuff in your mouth. The red velvet will melt your brain. *9635 Little Santa Monica Blvd. (2 blocks west of Rodeo Dr.), Beverly Hills. ☎ 310/274-8765. $.*

Head east on Santa Monica Blvd., north on La Cienega Blvd., and then west on Sunset Blvd.

⑧ Sunset Plaza. On the high-octane Sunset Strip, here's an oasis of chi-chi shopping, strolling, and outdoor snacking. Stars are drawn to designer boutiques such as Hugo Boss, Nicole Miller, Catherine Malandrino, and Calypso. Oliver Peoples sports eye-catching eyewear. Ole Henriksen Face/Body helps the beautiful people stay that way. If you're tiring of these trivial pursuits, shuffle a few blocks west to Book Soup, the best place in the city for browsing books.

Go west on Santa Monica Blvd., turn right on Seventh St., and then go right on Montana Ave.

Abbot Kinney Boulevard is known for its funky stores and eateries.

9 Montana Avenue. Next to a lovely Santa Monica neighborhood, these shops are all about maintaining the good life. There's Dermalogica and Kiehl's for skincare, the oft-imitated Shabby Chic, and plenty of children's clothing stores like Cranky Pants. Every Picture Tells a Story is a gallery for illustrators of children's books. High-end boutiques such as Morgan Le Fay and Jill Roberts are also a presence. *Montana Ave. (btwn Seventh & 17th sts.).*

Head 1 block west on Montana Ave., then go south on Lincoln Blvd. Go west at Ocean Park Blvd. to Main St.

10 Main Street, Santa Monica. This street's laid-back beach vibe makes the artsy discoveries even more surprising: There's Eames Office, with all things about the modernist designers; Obsolete Inc., with conversation-starting antiques; Arts and Letters's original stationary; Angel City's oodles of used books; and the Art Nouveau exterior of Paris 1900, which specializes in ladies finery from 1900 to 1930. *Main St. (btwn Pacific St. & Rose Ave.), Santa Monica.*

Take Main St. south, past Rose Ave., to Abbot Kinney Blvd.

11 ★ Abbot Kinney. An eclectic mix of funky art, health-conscious eats, and beach-chic decor—these shops are born of Venice's bohemian roots. Equator Books & Vinyl is a pulsing space with art, records, and out-of-print books. Strange Invisible Perfume can customize a scent for you. Unpretentious fashion boutiques include the Brit-themed Brick Lane, minimalist Salt, frothy Ecookie, eclectic Heist, and Stronghold's, a corral of denim Americana. Check out Surfing Cowboys for its retro surf home decor, and Turquoise for its fantastic vintage furniture. Jin Patisserie can help you wash it all down with tea and treats.

Take Abbot Kinney Blvd. south to Venice Blvd. and go east. At Lincoln Blvd., go north to I-10, head east, exit Maple Ave., and turn left.

12 Santee Alley. Do you enjoy haggling in seven languages? Is jostling your favorite hobby? Do you want a Louis Vuitton bag for 20 bucks that looks identical, I mean similar, to the one you couldn't afford on Rodeo Drive? If you say yes to any of these questions, this is your place. *In the alley btwn Maple Ave. & Santee St. (btwn Olympic Blvd. & 11th St.). Daily 10am–6pm.*

L.A. for **Architecture Fans**

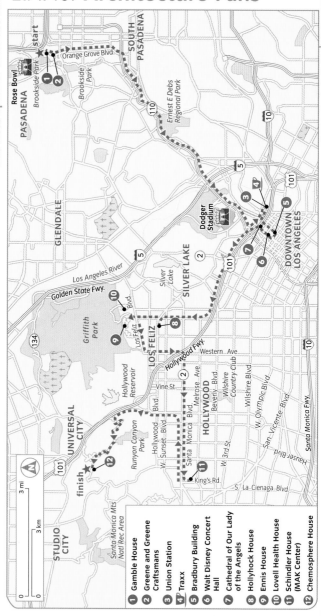

1 Gamble House
2 Greene and Greene Craftsmans
3 Union Station
4 Traxx
5 Bradbury Building
6 Walt Disney Concert Hall
7 Cathedral of Our Lady of the Angels
8 Hollyhock House
9 Ennis House
10 Lovell Health House
11 Schindler House (MAK Center)
12 Chemosphere House

This is a lot of architecture to digest: Pasadena's Craftsman bungalows, Downtown's mix of old and new classics, and prime examples of Californian modernism with Schindler, Neutra, and Lautner—the artistic offspring of Frank Lloyd Wright. START: **Pasadena.**

Take the 134 east, exit Orange Grove, and head north; turn left on Westmoreland Place.

1 ★★ **Gamble House.** This 1908 masterpiece in the American Art and Crafts style was designed by Charles and Henry Greene, brothers who built many stunning Craftsman bungalows in the Pasadena area. Commissioned by David and Mary Gamble (of Proctor and Gamble) to be their winter residence in California, the house is a National Historic Landmark. The exterior uses Japanese-style proportions, low and horizontal, in an open, Californian setting. The interior is especially impressive with stained-glass doors and windows, and intricately crafted woodwork. An extensive renovation in 2004 has preserved all of the home's immaculate details, and the hour-long tour is highly recommended. Movie fans might recognize the residence as Doc Brown's place in *Back to the Future.* ⏱ *1 hr. 4 Westmoreland Place, Pasadena.* ☎ *626/793-3334. www.gamble house.org. Tours Thurs–Sun noon–3pm. $10 adults, $7 seniors & students, free for kids under 12 when accompanied by an adult.*

2 **Greene and Greene Craftsmans.** Several excellent examples of the Greene and Greene architectural firm dot the streets of Arroyo Terrace and Grand Avenue (within walking distance of the Gamble House). Start at 2 Westmoreland Place with the Cole House, which is distinguishable by the river rock pillars of the carriage porch. Head south to Arroyo Terrace and check out nos. 440, 408, 400, and 370, and Charles Sumner Greene's own house at 368 Arroyo Terrace. Follow the road west to Grand Avenue and head south to find my favorite, the Duncan-Irwin House at 240 N. Grand Ave., and continue on to nos. 235 and 90. ⏱ *30 min. Arroyo Terrace & Grand Ave., Pasadena. Maps are available from the Gamble House bookstore. Note: None of these houses is open to the public.*

Go south on Orange Grove Blvd., then southwest on 110; exit Cesar E. Chavez Ave., and then head southeast to Alameda St.

3 **Union Station.** The trouble with being an architectural highlight in Los Angeles since 1939 is the risk of overexposure in film and television. You've seen Union Station in

The Gamble House in Pasadena is a National Historic Landmark.

Speed, Blade Runner, and *Bugsy,* more recently in the series *24,* and in countless other shows. This grand building combines elements of California Mission style with Streamline Moderne. The cathedral-size interior is lavishly detailed with colorful tiles, ornate wood paneling, retro leather chairs, and exposed roof beams. ⏱ *20 min. 800 N. Alameda St.* ☎ *213/683-6979. Open 24 hr.*

4 **Traxx.** Cool off at the bar at Traxx, probably the best restaurant you'll find in a train station. *800 N. Alameda St.* ☎ *213/625-1999. $$.*

Head north on Alameda St., turn left at Cesar E. Chavez Ave., and then go left at Broadway.

5 ★ **Bradbury Building.** The ordinary brick facade of this 1893 office building masks one of the most striking interior spaces you'll ever find. A peaked glass ceiling makes for a dramatic dance of sunlight and shadow in the five-story atrium, which has two open-cage elevators, suspended mail chutes, marble staircases, and spidery, wrought-iron railings. When the original architect, Sumner Hunt, was fired for boring his backer, Lewis Bradbury, the job was handed to an inexperienced draftsman named George Wyman, who took more inspiration from science fiction than from formal architectural training. ⏱ *20 min. 304 S. Broadway.* ☎ *213/626-1893. Mon–Fri 9am–6pm, Sat–Sun 9am–5pm.*

Head north on Broadway, and then turn left at First St. (Tom Bradley Blvd.).

6 ★★★ **Walt Disney Concert Hall.** Frank Gehry's instant classic is a Rorschach test for lovers of architecture. What do you see as you gaze upon its steel waves? Circle the 22 million pounds of steel and try to find an angle that doesn't stretch

your imagination like taffy. The audio tour narrated by John Lithgow is a great primer, but you'll have to come back for a show to experience the auditorium and its stunning acoustics. ⏱ *1 hr. 111 S. Grand Ave.* ☎ *323/850-2000. www.wdch.laphil. com. 45- to 60-min. audio tours most days, 10am–2pm. 45- to 60-min. guided tours Sat–Sun, times vary 10am–1pm. Free admission.*

Head north on Grand Ave., and then go right at Temple St.

7 ★ **Cathedral of Our Lady of the Angels.** In 2002, for the first time in 30 years, a new Roman Catholic cathedral was erected on U.S. soil, and it was designed by the Spanish architect José Rafael Moneo. With an ultramodern design that eschews right angles, the cathedral is the third largest in the world. ⏱ *20 min. 555 W. Temple St.* ☎ *213/680-5200. www.olacathedral. org. Mon–Fri 6:30am–6pm, Sat 9am–6pm, Sun 7am–6pm. Free organ recital Wed 12:45–1:15pm.*

Head northeast on Grand Ave. to US-101 N. Stay on 101 as it forks left; take exit 6A, Vermont Ave. Turn left on Hollywood Blvd.

8 **Hollyhock House.** The legendary Frank Lloyd Wright designed this private residence for oil heiress Aline Barnsdall, who envisioned it as the centerpiece of a large arts complex. The hilltop structure is modeled after a Maya temple, with exterior

Cathedral of Our Lady of the Angels.

A peek inside Frank Lloyd Wright's Hollyhock House.

walls tilting back slightly, and a roofline with symmetrical reliefs based on a geometric abstraction of the owner's favorite flower, the hollyhock. ⏱ *1 hr. 4800 Hollywood Blvd.* ☎ *323/644-6269. www.hollyhock house.net. Tours Wed–Sun 12:30, 1:30, 2:30 & 3:30pm. $7 adults, $3 students & seniors, free for children under 12.*

Head north on Vermont Ave. After Los Feliz Blvd. bear left at the fork onto Glendower Ave.

⑨ ★ **Ennis House.** Maya imagery is also visible in this 1924 building, the best and last of Frank Lloyd Wright's four "textile block" homes. Unfortunately, the house is aging poorly, no thanks to earthquakes and mudslides. Look, but don't touch. ⏱ *20 min. 2655 Glendower Ave.* ☎ *323/660-0607. www. ennishouse.org. Closed for repairs.*

Go east on Los Feliz Blvd., and then go north on Commonwealth Ave. Turn left onto Dundee Dr.

⑩ ★ **Lovell Health House.** This 1929 modernist masterpiece earned worldwide acclaim for Richard Neutra, an Austrian architect who worked briefly under Frank Lloyd Wright. Along with Rudolph Schindler's Lovell Beach House, the Lovell Health House came to be recognized as one of the first major examples of the International Style in the United States. ⏱ *20 min. 4616 Dundee Dr. Private residence; no tours.*

Head west on Los Feliz Blvd., south on Western Ave., west on Santa Monica Blvd., and then south on King's Rd.

⑪ ★ **Schindler House (MAK Center).** Another Austrian architect who worked under Frank Lloyd Wright, Rudolph Schindler came west to work on the Hollyhock House before launching his own practice with the design of his home in 1922. Modern and modular, with interlocking L shapes, the house was conceptualized as shared living and work space for multiple households. ⏱ *1 hr. 835 N. King's Rd.* ☎ *323/ 651-1510. www.makcenter.org. Wed– Sun 11am–6pm. $7 adults, $6 students & seniors, free children under 12. Free tours Sat–Sun 11am–6pm.*

Head east on Santa Monica Blvd., and then go north on Crescent Heights Blvd. Continue on Laurel Canyon Blvd.; turn right onto Mullholland Dr.

⑫ ★ **Chemosphere House.** No, it's not a flying saucer hovering on a hillside. It's an octagonal house perched atop a 5-foot-wide concrete column in the Hollywood Hills. Designed by the imaginative John Lautner in 1960, the house looks space-age and sunny, like a summer home for the Jetsons. Take a peek from Mulholland Drive or Torreyson Drive. ⏱ *20 min. 7776 Torreyson Dr. Private residence; no tours.*

Museum Row

1. La Brea Bakery
2. Petersen Automotive Museum
3. Craft and Folk Art Museum
4. Page Museum at La Brea Tar Pits
5. Los Angeles County Museum of Art (LACMA)

Museum Row is a nifty cluster of four museums, all within a few hundred yards of each other. We'll debunk two myths about Los Angeles: That there's no walking and no culture. **With the exception of La Brea Bakery, these stops are within walking distance of one another.**

---

1 **La Brea Bakery.** Not far from Museum Row is this outstanding bakery created by Nancy Silverton. Choosing between scones—ginger or maple walnut?—torments me. They also have great coffee, sandwiches with artisanal cheeses, and sidewalk tables. *624 S. La Brea Ave., at Wilshire Blvd.* ☎ *323/939-6813. $.*

Head west on Wilshire Blvd.

2 ★ kids **Petersen Automotive Museum.** There could be no better city than Los Angeles to

house a museum about the automobile and how it's shaped the American culture. And the museum's not just for Ferrari fetishists who wash their car daily with a diaper. Founded by Robert Petersen of *Hot Rod* and *Motor Trend* magazines, the four-story museum features more than 200 cars. Past exhibitions have included "Microcars," "The American Convertible," "Alternative Power," "Cars and Guitars," "Muscle Cars," and "Heads of State." There's an ongoing exhibition of Hollywood star cars, including the original 1966 Batmobile and a 1942 Cadillac that

One of the many sweet rides on display at the Petersen Automotive Museum.

Clark Gable gave to his wife, Carole Lombard. Kids flock to the Discovery Center, where they can learn about how a car works with Professor Lugnut or hop on a police motorcycle in the Vroom Room. ⏱ *1 hr. 6060 Wilshire Blvd., at Fairfax Ave.* ☎ *323/930-CARS. www.petersen. org. $10 adults, $5 seniors & students, $3 children 5–12, free for kids under 5. Tues–Sun 10am–6pm. Parking $5.*

❸ Craft and Folk Art Museum. Running the gamut between traditional folk art and contemporary arts and crafts, this museum offers exhibits far off the beaten path: Aboriginal art from Balgo, Australia; dioramas of a multi-generational circus family; Palestinian embroidery; Carnaval headdresses; and images of Haitian voodoo gods. The museum shop

Museum of Contemporary Art (MOCA)

Dedicated to art from 1940 to the present, MOCA's permanent collection contains 5,000 pieces, including work by Andy Warhol, Jasper Johns, Robert Rauschenberg, Willem de Koonig, Nan Goldin, Mark Rothko, Cy Twombly, and David Hockney. The museum's superb reputation derives from its sparkling temporary exhibitions; in recent years the museum hit gold with catchy retrospectives on Warhol and Basquiat. On Saturday nights in the summer, a program called MOCA After Dark draws artsy hipsters with a lively mix of DJ music, spoken word, art workshops, and film screenings. Two other MOCA outposts can be found in Little Tokyo (152 N. Central Ave.) and West Hollywood (8687 Melrose Ave.). *250 S. Grand Ave.* ☎ *213/626-6222. www.moca.org. $8 adults, $5 seniors & students, free for children under 12. Free for all Thurs 5–8pm. Mon & Fri 11am–5pm, Thurs 11am–8pm, Sat–Sun 11am–6pm.*

At the Museum of Contemporary Art (MOCA).

has some fantastic items such as clutch purses made from recycled Mexican candy wrappers, and, my favorite, hand-blown gin bottles found by Java fishermen after being tossed by Dutch sailors a couple centuries prior. ⏱ *30 min. 5814 Wilshire Blvd. (btwn Fairfax & La Brea aves.).* ☎ *323/937-4230. www. cafam.org. $10 adults, $5 seniors & students, free for children under 12. Free for all 1st Wed of the month. Museum exhibits Wed–Sun 11am–5pm; museum shop Tues–Sun 11am–5pm.*

4 ★ **kids Page Museum at La Brea Tar Pits.** In a town that's not always reverential toward history (much less prehistory), the La Brea Tar Pits capture life as it was in the Los Angeles Basin tens of thousands of years ago. About 10 gallons a day still oozes to the surface and occasionally will trap a bird or lizard or an over-eager tourist (just kidding). The first written account of the asphalt seepage was in 1770 by a Franciscan friar, who theorized that the goo was the cause of the area's earthquakes. Native Americans used the sticky substance for thousands of years as waterproof caulking for baskets and canoes. ⏱ *1 hr. 5801 Wilshire Blvd.* ☎ *323/934-7243. www.tarpits.org. Mon–Fri 9:30am–5pm, Sat–Sun 10am–5pm. $7 adults, $4.50 seniors & students, $2 kids 5–12, free for kids under 5.*

5 ★★★ **kids Los Angeles County Museum of Art (LACMA).** The city's largest collection of art (with 110,000 pieces) is spread across a hodgepodge of buildings from different eras. Since 2004 the staff has worked with internationally acclaimed architect Renzo Piano to create a master plan that unifies and beautifies the LACMA campus. The initial phase should be completed sometime in 2008; this includes the underground parking, BP Grand Entrance, and the Broad Contemporary Art Museum. *See the minitour on p 43.*

Camille Pissarro's Place du Théâtre Français *(1898).*

LACMA

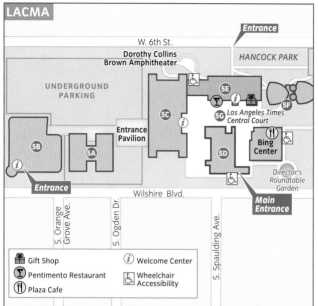

Map labels:
- W. 6th St.
- Entrance
- HANCOCK PARK
- Dorothy Collins Brown Amphitheater
- UNDERGROUND PARKING
- 5E
- 5C
- Los Angeles Times Central Court
- 5G
- 5F
- Entrance Pavilion
- 5B
- 5A
- Bing Center
- 5D
- Director's Roundtable Garden
- Entrance
- Wilshire Blvd.
- Main Entrance
- S. Orange Grove Ave.
- S. Ogden Dr.
- S. Spaulding Ave.

Legend:
- 🎁 Gift Shop
- 🍸 Pentimento Restaurant
- 🍽 Plaza Cafe
- ⓘ Welcome Center
- ♿ Wheelchair Accessibility

Start at the **5A** **Broad Contemporary Art Museum,** which is the new home of the museum's 20th-century paintings and sculptures, including work by Hockney, Kadinsky, Magritte, and Matisse. If you're with kids, head next door to the **5B** **LACMA West** (in the 1939 Art Deco building that used to be the May Company department store) to play in the Boone Children's Gallery, where kids can make art of their own. Head back to the entrance and continue on to the **5C** **Ahmanson Building,** where you can meander for days in an astounding array of galleries: Chinese, Korean, African, Islamic, pre-Columbian, South and Southeast Asian, European Painting, and the Decorative Arts. On the south side of the courtyard is the **5D** **Art of the Americas Building,** which has the American and Latin American collections. Here you'll find work by Winslow Homer (The Cotton Pickers), Mary Cassat (Mother About to Wash Her Sleepy Child), and Diego Rivera. The **5E** **Hammer Building,** just north across the courtyard, houses 19th-century European art, Impressionism and Post-Impressionism, and photography by Walker Evans, Alfred Stieglitz, Diane Arbus, and more. Next door to the east, the serene **5F** **Japanese Pavilion** displays Buddhist and Shinto sculpture, woodblock prints, Edo paintings, and intricately carved sculptures called netsuke. Time your visit to catch the free **5G** **Friday Night Jazz** series, which features Californian jazz artists playing in the courtyard (Apr–Nov Fri 6–8pm). ⏰ *2–3 hr. 5905 Wilshire Blvd.* ☎ *323/857-6000. www.lacma. org. Mon–Tues & Thurs noon–8pm, Fri noon–9pm, Sat–Sun 11am–8pm. $9 adults, $5 seniors & students, free for kids under 18. Free for all after 5pm & all day the 2nd Tues of the month. Parking $5–$8.*

Rockin' L.A.

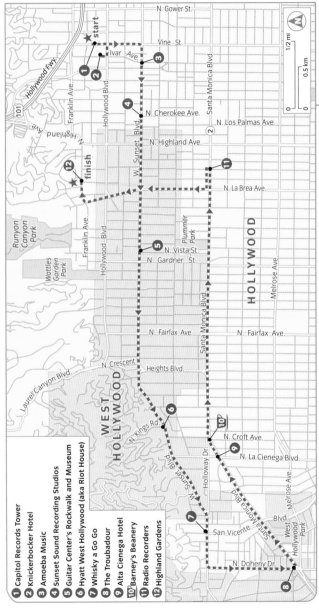

1. Capitol Records Tower
2. Knickerbocker Hotel
3. Amoeba Music
4. Sunset Sound Recording Studios
5. Guitar Center's Rockwalk and Museum
6. Hyatt West Hollywood (aka Riot House)
7. Whisky a Go Go
8. The Troubadour
9. Alta Cienega Hotel
10. Barney's Beanery
11. Radio Recorders
12. Highland Gardens

This tour will take you through the heart and history of the Los Angeles music scene—the good, the bad, and the ugly. Ratchet up the attitude, don your shades, and strut. Let the city be your mix CD: "Good Vibrations" by The Beach Boys, "L.A. Woman" by The Doors, "Hotel California" by The Eagles, "Los Angeles" by X, "I Love L.A." by Randy Newman, "Valley Girl" by Frank and Moon Zappa, "Walking in L.A." by The Missing Persons, "Welcome to the Jungle" by Guns N' Roses, "Angeles" by Elliot Smith, and Tupac's "California Love." START: **Just north of Hollywood Boulevard and Vine Street.**

❶ ★ Capitol Records Tower.

Two blocks north of the world-famous corner of Hollywood and Vine is the landmark that Hollywood loves to demolish—at least in its disaster movies *(Earthquake, The Day After Tomorrow)*. The 13-story structure might look like a gigantic stack of vinyl 45 records on a turntable (a heap of mp3s doesn't have the same magic, does it?), but it was actually designed by Modernist architect Welton Becket to be the world's first circular building when it debuted in 1956. Frank Sinatra banged out 19 albums in these hallowed studios, which also recorded the likes of Nat King Cole, Ella Fitzgerald, Dean Martin, and The Beach Boys. The first record company based on the west coast, Capitol Records also imported British acts such as Pink Floyd, Duran Duran, Radiohead, and The Beatles. On the sidewalk in front of the building's lobby, you can find John Lennon's Hollywood star, which is still decorated by fans every December 8 to commemorate the anniversary of his death. 🕐 *20 min. 1750 Vine St.* ☎ *323/462-6252.*

One block west of Hollywood Blvd. and Vine St.

❷ Knickerbocker Hotel.

Could this unassuming senior home be the original Heartbreak Hotel? While in town shooting his film debut in "Love Me Tender," Elvis Presley stayed in room no. 1016 of the storied Knickerbocker Hotel and found inspiration

Amoeba Music is L.A.'s best independent record store.

for his hit song "Heartbreak Hotel," (which he cowrote). 🕐 *10 min. 1714 Ivar St.* ☎ *323/962-8898.*

Head south on Vine St., and then go west on Sunset Blvd.

❸ ★ Amoeba Music.

A mecca for music lovers, this independently owned store spans an entire block of Sunset, and offers the biggest and baddest selection of tunes in town. It's also an intimate live venue; recently featured was an unannounced set by an up-and-comer named Sir Paul McCartney. 🕐 *1 hr. 6400 Sunset Blvd.* ☎ *323/245-6400. www.amoeba.com. Mon–Sat 10:30am–11pm, Sun 11am–9pm.*

❹ Sunset Sound Recording Studios.

It may be impossible to

Blondie solidifies its place in history at Hollywood's Rockwalk.

find a recording studio that's got more musical mojo than Sunset Sound: It's turned out 200 gold records, including *Led Zeppelin II* and *Led Zeppelin IV*, Michael Jackson's *Thriller*, The Beach Boys' *Pet Sounds*, The Rolling Stones' *Exile on Main Street*, as well as albums by Bob Dylan, Van Halen, Fleetwood Mac, and Beck. ⏱ *10 min. 6650 Sunset Blvd.* ☎ *323/469-1186. www. sunsetsound.com.*

⑤ Guitar Center's Rockwalk and Museum. The Rockwalk, the sidewalk in front of the Guitar Center, is the rock equivalent of the forecourt of Grauman's Chinese Theatre. The concrete has been high-fived by the talented hands of Chuck Berry, Jerry Lee Lewis, Jimmy Page, Eddie Van Halen, and many others. There's also an awesome display of memorabilia such as Eddie's home-made red Kramer guitar, Stevie Ray Vaughn's denim jacket, Keith Moon's drum kit, and platform boots from KISS. Oh yeah, you can buy a guitar here, too. ⏱ *1 hr. 7425 Sunset Blvd.* ☎ *323/874-1060. www.rockwalk. com. Mon–Fri 10am–9pm, Sat 10am–8pm, Sun 11am–8pm.*

⑥ Hyatt West Hollywood (aka Riot House). This monument to mayhem began life innocently enough in 1958 as the Gene Autry Hotel. By the mid-'60s, the name had changed to the Continental Hyatt, and the hotel became the stomping grounds (literally) of rock-'n'-rollers who came to play nearby clubs on the Strip. Over the years the Riot House, as it came to be called, became a sort of bad-boy finishing school; members of Led Zeppelin rode their motorcycles up and down the hallways, and, on separate occasions, Keith Richards of The Rolling Stones and Keith Moon of The Who hurled televisions out of 10th-floor windows. ⏱ *10 min. 8401 Sunset Blvd.* ☎ *323/656-1234.*

⑦ ★ Whisky a Go Go. Aside from its footnote as the birthplace of go-go dancing, the Whisky opened in 1964 and was the epicenter of the Los Angeles rock scene for three decades. The 1960s saw The Doors, The Byrds, Love, and Buffalo Springfield. The 1970s imported Led Zeppelin, The Who, and Roxy Music. The lineup in the later '70s edged toward the home-grown punk rock of The Germs, The Runaways, and X. Then came the pop metal of Van Halen, followed by Mötley Crüe, and Guns N' Roses in the '80s. In 2007 the reunited Police polished their chops at the revered Whisky before embarking on their worldwide tour. ⏲ *10 min. 8901 W. Sunset Blvd., at Clark St.* ☎ *310/ 652-4202. www.whiskyagogo.com.*

Head west on Sunset Blvd., and then go south on Doheny Dr. to Santa Monica Blvd.

8 ★ **The Troubadour.** In the 1960s the Troubadour was a hotbed for folkies such as Bob Dylan and Joni Mitchell. Over the years, the small club helped launch the careers of other singer-songwriters: James Taylor, Elton John, Randy Newman, and Tom Waits. And in 1985, during the heyday of heavy metal, Guns N' Roses made its debut on this stage and caught the eye of a Geffen A&R rep. My favorite "wish-I-was-there" moment happened in 1974, when John Lennon (on his 18-month-long "lost weekend" in Los Angeles) and Harry Nilsson were tossed out for getting drunk and heckling the Smothers Brothers. ⏲ *10 min. 9081 Santa Monica Blvd.* ☎ *310/276-6168. www.troubadour.com.*

Take Santa Monica Blvd. east to La Cienega Blvd.

9 **Alta Cienega Motel.** From 1968 to 1970, Jim Morrison lived in room no. 32. Today its walls are graffitied with messages from adoring fans who rent a piece of history for a night or two. ⏲ *10 min. 1005 N. La Cienega Ave.* ☎ *310/652-5797. www.altacienegamotel.com.*

Continue 2 blocks east on Santa Monica Blvd.

George Harrison, Jayne Mansfield, and John Lennon at Whisky a Go Go in 1964.

10 **Barney's Beanery.** In the late '60s and early '70s, this restaurant and bar drew local rockers with its roadhouse loosey-gooseness. With The Doors' offices and studio practically next door, it was one of Jim Morrison's favorite spots to eat, drink, and hold court. Regular Janis Joplin preferred booth 34, where she knocked back a few on the night she died. *8447 Santa Monica Blvd.* ☎ *323/654-2287. www.barneys beanery.com. $.*

Take Santa Monica Blvd east.

11 **Radio Recorders.** Elvis Presley rocked the walls here throughout the 1950s, recording more than 100 songs, including the hits—weren't they all hits?—"All Shook Up," "Jailhouse Rock," and "Love Me Tender." ⏲ *10 min. 7000 Santa Monica Blvd. No phone.*

Take Santa Monica Blvd. west to La Brea Ave. and go north; then go east on Franklin Ave.

12 **Highland Gardens.** On October 4, 1970, Janis Joplin partied at the Troubadour and Barney's Beanery (see above), then went back to her room (no. 105), and accidentally overdosed on heroin. ⏲ *10 min. 7047 Franklin Ave.* ☎ *323/850-0536. www.highlandgardenshotel.com.*

I See Dead People

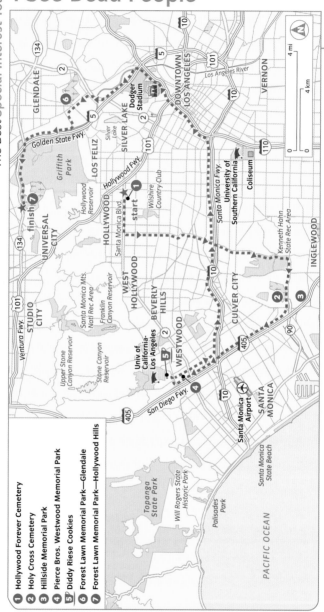

1 Hollywood Forever Cemetery
2 Holy Cross Cemetery
3 Hillside Memorial Park
4 Pierce Bros. Westwood Memorial Park
5 Diddy Riese Cookies
6 Forest Lawn Memorial Park—Glendale
7 Forest Lawn Memorial Park—Hollywood Hills

For those people who prefer their celebrity-seeking to be a tad more predictable, here's a tour of a few fallen stars and their favorite final hangouts. And this should go without saying: Please be respectful.

① ★★ Hollywood Forever Cemetery.

The oldest graveyard in L.A., Hollywood Forever was established in 1899 on 100 green acres (40 of which were sold in 1920 to Paramount Pictures, which remains there today). By the 1930s, this was *the* hot resting spot for Hollywood's movers and shakers. On the day Rudolph Valentino's casket was carried into the mausoleum, 80,000 fans jammed onto the grounds to get a glimpse of the fallen star. The manager from 1939 to 1995, Jules Roth, proved to be shadier than the park's tree-lined paths, and over the years he let the grounds deteriorate into a maze of weeds, potholes, and graffiti; he even sold off property to strip-mall developers (which explains the cemetery's less-than-idyllic curb appeal). In 1998, facing bankruptcy and then the auction block, Hollywood Forever was staring death in the eye. Enter a young man named Tyler Cassity, who bought it for $375,000 and brought it back to life by sinking millions more into renovation and repairs. But a cemetery's reputation lives and dies by the names of those who are buried there, so let's call roll: Cecil B. DeMille; John Huston; Douglas Fairbanks, Sr.; Peter Lorre; Jayne Mansfield; Benjamin "Bugsy" Siegel; "Alfalfa" and "Darla" from the Little Rascals; Mel Blanc; and all three Talmadge sisters. The cemetery is also the home of two Ramones, Johnny and Dee Dee; since 2005 Johnny's wife Linda has hosted an annual Ramones Memorial, which, in previous years, featured the screening of Ramones documentaries and the unveiling of a larger-than-life bronze statue of Johnny Ramone rocking out. 🕐 1–2 hr. 6000 Santa Monica Blvd., at Gower St. ☎ 323/469-1181. www.hollywoodforever.com. Daily 7am–7pm.

Head west on Santa Monica Blvd., south on La Brea Ave., and then west on Slauson Ave.

② Holy Cross Cemetery.

This Roman Catholic cemetery is sprawling (nearly 200 acres), so you might want to do a combination of driving and walking. After entering from Slauson Avenue, follow the left road up the hill; you'll reach a grotto that has the graves of Bing Crosby, Bela Lugosi, Rita Hayworth, Jimmy Durante, Jackie Coogan, and Sharon Tate and her unborn child. Elsewhere

An adoring fan visits the memorial of Johnny Ramone at the Hollywood Forever Cemetery.

The hard-to-miss Al Jolson memorial at Hillside Memorial Park.

on the grounds of Holy Cross are Mack Sennet, John Ford, Rosalind Russell, and Lawrence Welk. In the mausoleum are Fred MacMurray, Ray Bolger, and John Candy. 🕐 *30 min. 5835 W. Slauson Ave.* ☎ *310/670-7697. Mon–Fri 8am–5pm, Sat 8am–4pm, Sun 10am–4pm.*

Head east on Slauson Ave.; turn right on Buckingham Pkwy., left on Green Valley Circle, and then right on Centinela Ave.

❸ **Hillside Memorial Park.** This Jewish cemetery is one of the most welcoming to fans and happily provides a map upon request. The biggies here include Jack Benny, Milton Berle, Max Factor, Philip and Julius Epstein (twin brothers who wrote *Casablanca*), Moe Howard, Michael Landon, Lorne Green, Vic Morrow, Dinah Shore, and Shelly Winters. The cemetery's splashiest attraction is the Al Jolson monument, which features a 120-foot, cascading waterfall; a white-marble dome held by six pillars; and a statue of Jolson on one knee, a la the "Mammy!" song from *The Jazz Singer*. 🕐 *30 min. 6001 W. Centinela Ave.* ☎ *310/641-070. Sun–Fri 8am–5pm.*

Head east on Centinela Ave., and then go right on La Tijera Blvd. to 405 north; exit Wilshire Blvd., and go right on Glendon Ave.

❹ **Pierce Bros. Westwood Memorial Park.** In Westwood, near the U.C.L.A. campus, this little 3-acre cemetery is half hidden by the high-rises on Wilshire Boulevard. It may be a little confusing to find (enter on Glendon Ave., just south of Wilshire Blvd.), but the great thing is that you can cover it all with an easy stroll. Make a beeline for Marilyn Monroe in the northeast corner. She made the place fashionable in 1962; since then the cemetery has welcomed Dean Martin, Natalie Wood, Donna Reed, John Cassavetes, Roy Orbison, Don Knotts, Jack Lemmon, Walter Matthau, George C. Scott, Burt Lancaster, Bob Crane, Truman Capote, Billy Wilder, Buddy Rich, Rodney Dangerfield, Mel Tormé (a bright red grave!), and Darryl F. Zannuck. Peter Lawford was a tenant here too, until he was

tossed out; apparently, the mortu-
ary bills went unpaid, and his fourth
wife had to scatter the ashes in the
Pacific Ocean. ⏲ *1 hr. 1218 Glendon
Ave., Westwood.* ☎ *310/474-1579.
Daily 8am–sundown.*

Head north on Glendon Ave., take
a left at Weyborn Ave., and then
turn right at Broxton Ave.

5 Diddy Riese Cookies. A sugar
boost might help you make the
cross-town drive. Line up among the
U.C.L.A. students for an ice-cream
sandwich that costs a buck and a
quarter at this Westwood Village
mainstay. *926 Broxton Ave., at Le
Conte Ave.* ☎ *310/208-0448. $.*

Go south on 405, east on I-10,
north on 110 toward Pasadena,
and then north on I-5 toward
Sacramento; exit CA-2 toward
Glendale, and then exit San Fernando Rd. and turn left at San
Fernando Rd. Take a right at Glendale Ave.

**6 Forest Lawn Memorial
Park—Glendale.** In both size and
status, this is the big daddy of Los

*Marilyn Monroe's crypt at the Pierce
Bros. Westwood Memorial Park is a
popular stop for her fans.*

Angeles cemeteries. Some of the
biggest names from Hollywood's
Golden Age rest in peace among
these 300 acres of lush rolling hills,
spotted with old-world architecture
and art, including replicas of
Michelangelo's greatest works and a
stained-glass re-creation of da Vinci's
The Last Supper. Unfortunately,

Cinespia

No one with a pulse can resist a classic movie projected on a
mausoleum wall. Classic and campy, creepy and cool—Cinespia is a
summer screening series set on the tomb-strewn grounds of the Hollywood Forever Cemetery. With rabid word-of-mouth and national
press coverage (*Vanity Fair, USA Today,* and *NPR*), the scene at this
boneyard is anything but underground. Pack a picnic basket and get
there early to claim a choice spot (or is it plot?) on the grass and enjoy
a glass of wine as the sun sets and the DJ spins. Parking and entrance
can be a slog, but the crowd's enthusiasm—cheering a crackling line
from Cary Grant or Jack Nicholson—is downright refreshing. *6000
Santa Monica Blvd., at Gower St. www.cinespia.org. Sat in the summer, gates open at 7:30pm, film begins at 9pm. Admission $10.*

At the entrance to Forest Lawn Memorial Park–Hollywood Hills.

Forest Lawn discourages sightseers. Many tombs are in private gardens or mausoleums and are not accessible; these include those of Humphrey Bogart, Mary Pickford, Clark Gable, Carole Lombard, Harold Lloyd, Nat King Cole, Clara Bow, George Burns and Gracie Allen, and W. C. Fields. But here are some names that you *can* find if you keep moving: Jimmy Stewart, Spencer Tracy, Walt Disney, Errol Flynn, Edith Head, Ernst Lubitsch, Theodore Dreiser, and Aimee Semple McPherson. ⏱ *1 hr. 1712 S. Glendale Ave., Glendale.* ☎ *323/254-3131. www. forestlawn.com. Daily 8am–6pm.*

Head north on San Fernando Rd., west on Los Feliz Blvd., north on I-5, and west on CA-134 toward Ventura, and then exit at Forest Lawn.

❼ Forest Lawn Memorial Park—Hollywood Hills. In 1948 Forest Lawn expanded onto 400 acres adjacent to Griffith Park on hills overlooking the studios of Warner Brothers and Disney. While the Hollywood Hills branch may have fewer stars than the original in Glendale, at least they are accessible (as long as you don't ask for any help from the staff). The grounds are gargantuan, so don't count on hunting down too many of these: Bette Davis, Lucille Ball, Buster Keaton, Liberace, Freddie Prinze, Andy Gibb, Jack Webb, Ernie Kovacs, Stan Laurel, Ozzie and Harriet Nelson, Ricky Nelson, Gene Autry, and Steve Allen. Before all the dead folks were here, D. W. Griffith shot the action sequences for his 1915 Civil War epic *The Birth of a Nation* here. ⏱ *1 hr. 6300 Forest Lawn Dr.* ☎ *323/254-3131. www.forestlawn.com. Daily 8am–5pm.* ●

Downtown

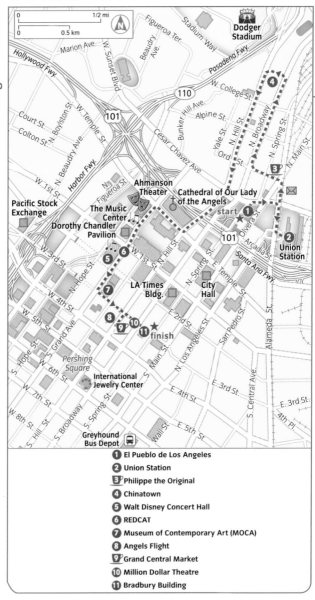

1 El Pueblo de Los Angeles
2 Union Station
3 Philippe the Original
4 Chinatown
5 Walt Disney Concert Hall
6 REDCAT
7 Museum of Contemporary Art (MOCA)
8 Angels Flight
9 Grand Central Market
10 Million Dollar Theatre
11 Bradbury Building

Previous page: In-line skaters liven up the crowds at Venice Beach.

Downtown Los Angeles has seen a remarkable resurgence in recent years and shows no signs of slowing down. Old architectural marvels (City Hall, the Orpheum, and the Eastern Columbia, to name a few) have been gussied up, while new marvels (Walt Disney Concert Hall and Cathedral of Our Lady of Angels, for example) have been added. Every week it seems another über-hip bar opens Downtown. START: **If you don't wish to drive Downtown, take the Metro Red Line from Hollywood/Highland to Union Station.**

1 ★ El Pueblo de Los Angeles. As the birthplace of Los Angeles, this makes an *excelente* start to a Downtown tour. Forty-four Mexican settlers founded a pueblo in 1781 on the orders of Carlos III of Spain, who needed food for the troops guarding Alta California, this faraway Spanish province. The 44-acre historical park contains the city's oldest house, **Avila Adobe** (1818); the city's oldest church, **Old Plaza Church** (1822); and the city's first fire station, **Old Plaza Firehouse** (1884). Wander the brick path of **Olvera Street,** a pedestrian marketplace bursting like a piñata with Mexican knickknacks. Keep an eye out for the **Pelanconi House** (1855), the first brick building in Los Angeles, and home to the popular **La Golondrina** restaurant since 1930. The visitor center is located in a Victorian building from 1887 called the **Sepulveda House,** where tours, maps, brochures, and

Olvera Street is teeming with colorful souvenirs.

gifts are available, as well as a free screening of a short film, *Pueblo of Promise*. *Visitor center: 622 N. Main St.* ☎ *213/628-1274. www.cityofla. org/ELP. Mon–Sat 10am–3pm. Most historic buildings: Mon–Sat 10am–3pm. Olvera St. market: daily 10am–7pm. La Golondrina restaurant: daily 9am–9pm.*

2 ★ Union Station. Considered to be the last great railway station built in America, this 1939 terminal used to see 7,000 folks a day, coming and going on three different railroads. Although it still serves as a vital transportation hub (subway, light rail, Metrolink, and Amtrak all stop here), today the station is better known as a time capsule of the golden age of train travel. A quiet seat in the glamorous waiting room—a cathedral ceiling, twinkling chandeliers, marble and tile finishes—is a trip back in time. *800 N. Alameda St.* ☎ *213/683-6979. Open 24 hr.*

3 Philippe the Original. Since the legendary eatery opened its doors a century ago, the big seller has been the French-dipped sandwich, which the restaurant claims to have invented (after taking a bite, you're not going to question it). With sawdust floors and dirt-cheap prices, legendary Philippe is an everyman's paradise. And just to prove that they're keeping it real, a cup of joe is a dime—you heard right: 10¢. *1001 N. Alameda St., at Ord St.* ☎ *213/ 628-3781. Daily 6am–10pm. $.*

Head west on Ord St. past the Jade Pavilion, and turn right on Broadway. Head north to Central Plaza at 947 N. Broadway.

4 **Chinatown.** Lacking the scope and vibrancy of the Chinese communities in San Francisco or New York, the "new" Chinatown—sadly, the "old" Chinatown was razed to make way for Union Station—juxtaposes a reverence for ancient traditions with an appreciation for the vanguard, such as the experimental art galleries blossoming on Chung King Road. Poke through the tiny shops in Central Plaza, and look for my favorite building, the Hop Louie Restaurant, a 1941 structure with a five-tier pagoda roof. Serenity seekers can visit the lovely new Buddhist temple, Cam Au, a few blocks away at 750 Yale St. *www.chinatownla.com.*

Just east of the intersection of Broadway and Ord St. is a DASH bus stop. For 25¢, Route B (or, on weekends, the DD) will take you to Grand Ave. and First St.

5 ★★★ **Walt Disney Concert Hall.** Frank Gehry's masterpiece is often credited with revitalizing Downtown L.A., but few residents appreciate its long and expensive road to fruition. Lillian Disney, Walt's widow, began the process in 1987 with a gift of $50 million. After the construction of a $100-million underground parking garage, fundraising took a hit with a real-estate depression in the early '90s. Groundbreaking finally took place in 1999, and construction was completed in 2003. The final tab came to $275 million. *111 S. Grand Ave.* ☎ *323/850-2000. www.laphil.com. 45- to 60-min. audio tours most days 10am–2pm. 45- to 60-min. guided tours Sat–Sun, times vary 10am–1pm. Free admission.*

6 **REDCAT.** Tucked away in the southwest corner of the Walt Disney Concert Hall, the Roy and Edna Disney/CalArts Theatre presents experimental films, plays, and art exhibitions. Equally provocative is the lounge's signature drink, the Cat-a-tonic. *631 W. Second St.* ☎ *213/237-2800. Tues–Fri 9am–9pm, Sat–Sun noon–9pm.*

Head south on Grand Ave.

7 ★★ **Museum of Contemporary Art (MOCA).** In a striking red sandstone building designed by acclaimed Japanese architect Arata Isozaki, this collection is a must-see for fans of the modern masters such as Warhol, Pollock, Rothko, and

Union Station in Downtown Los Angeles.

Spices, grains, produce, and unusual ingredients of all kinds are on offer at the Grand Central Market.

Lichtenstein. *250 S. Grand Ave.* ☎ *213/626-6222. www.moca.org. $8 adults, $5 seniors & students, free for children under 12. Free for all Thurs 5–8pm. Mon & Fri 11am–5pm, Thurs 11am–8pm, Sat–Sun 11am–6pm.*

Head east on Third St. to Hill St.

⑧ Angels Flight. The "shortest railway in the world" (actually a two-car funicular) was built in 1901 so that the wealthy residents of the Victorian mansions of Bunker Hill could take a penny ride down to the town's main shopping district. Eventually the well-heeled headed for the suburbs and the Bunker Hill enclave degenerated into slums; by 1969, the cars were put into storage. In 1996, after a 27-year hiatus, the Los Angeles landmark was restored and reopened; unfortunately, a fatal accident in 2001 shut it down once again. City preservationists are currently fighting to get Angels Flight back on track in coming years as a symbol of Downtown's revitalization. *Hill St. (btwn Third & Fourth sts.).*

Head across Hill St. to S. Broadway.

⑨ Grand Central Market. Since 1917 the open-air market has provided a lively, if sometimes chaotic, place to pick up coffee, ice cream, or tasty ethnic grub on the cheap—Hawaiian BBQ, Cuban sandwiches, Persian kebabs, pupusas, and empanadas. *317 S. Broadway.* ☎ *213/624-2378. www.grand centralsquare.com. $.*

⑩ Million Dollar Theatre. Built for a cost of (gasp!) $1 million, Sid Grauman's first take on a movie palace opened in 1918 with Mary Pickford and Charlie Chaplin on hand. The lavishly ornamented interior resembles a Mexican cathedral; in fact, for years a Spanish-speaking church held services in the 2,100-seat auditorium. Other spectacular theaters along the once-mighty Broadway District include the Los Angeles Theatre (615 S. Broadway), the Palace (630 S. Broadway), and the Orpheum (842 S. Broadway). *307 S. Broadway. Currently undergoing renovation.*

⑪ Bradbury Building. The city's oldest commercial building (built in 1893) contains an awe-inspiring courtyard, which has starred in numerous films, most memorably *Blade Runner. 304 S. Broadway.* ☎ *213/626-1893. Mon–Fri 9am–6pm, Sat–Sun 9am–5pm.*

The Best Neighborhood Walks

Venice

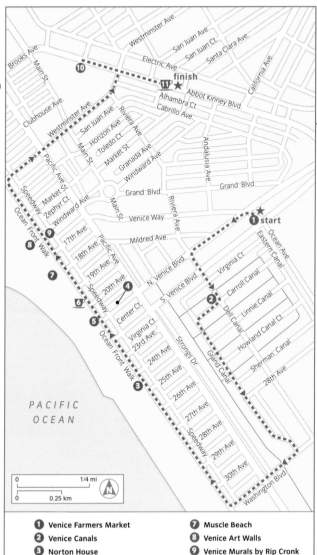

1 Venice Farmers Market
2 Venice Canals
3 Norton House
4 L.A. Louver
5 Venice Boardwalk
6 Jody Maroni's Sausage Kingdom
7 Muscle Beach
8 Venice Art Walls
9 Venice Murals by Rip Cronk
10 Abbot Kinney
11 Jin Patisserie

No area of the sprawling Los Angeles metropolis has as colorful a history as Venice. Before it was a place, it was a grand concept: first the "Coney Island of the Pacific," then "Venice of America." At the end of the 1920s, it was an oil boom town; a few years later, it was a ghost town. The '50s brought the Beatniks; the '60s, the hippies; the '70s, the surfers and skateboarders. In recent years, as the canals cleaned up and real estate soared, Venice has somehow managed to maintain its bohemian edge. START: **The first stop on this tour is open on Friday only. If you're visiting on another day, begin with ❷.**

❶ **Venice Farmers Market.** A morning stroll through a farmers market is a quintessential southern California experience. While Venice's market may not be the city's best (that title goes to Santa Monica's on Wed and Sat), it's friendly and brimming with adventurous fruits and vegetables like persimmons and squash blossoms. *502 Venice Blvd., at Venice Way. www.venicefarmers market.com. Fri 7–11am.*

Head west on Venice Blvd., and then south on Dell Ave.

❷ ★ **Venice Canals.** Only 6 canals remain of the original 16 that were built in 1904 by Abbot Kinney in his elaborate quest to build his ill-fated and short-lived European-style resort. Most of the canals were paved over in 1929 to make room for automobiles, while the few remaining canals were neglected for half a century. In 1994 the city dredged the canals and added small bridges and sidewalks. Tossing a few crumbs to the ducks in the placid water, you might wonder whether Kinney's vision was so crazy after all.

Head south on Grand Canal, and then west on Washington Blvd. Head north on Ocean Front Walk.

❸ **Norton House.** This residential design by Frank Gehry fascinates me, mainly because of its awfulness, as if a 9-year-old boy replaced the blueprints with his crayon sketch of

The eye-catching Norton House.

a treehouse. If, however, you side with the architect's opinion that "buildings under construction look nicer than buildings finished," you'll love this. *2509 Ocean Front Walk.*

❹ **L.A. Louver.** The 8,000-square-foot gallery displays the work of established contemporary artists like David Hockney and Ed Moses, as well as cutting-edge up-and-comers. *45 N. Venice Blvd. ☎ 310/ 822-4955. www.lalouver.com. Tues– Sat 10am–6pm. Free admission.*

5 ★★★ **Venice Boardwalk.** In most places, it's not polite to stare, but on the boardwalk, it's the highest compliment you can pay a performer (without actually *paying* a performer). The endless stream of tacky shops are perfect for buying gifts for (a) someone with a sense of humor, or (b) someone you don't really like. *Ocean Front Walk (btwn Venice Blvd. & Rose Ave.).*

6 ★ **Jody Maroni's Sausage Kingdom.** Although Jody Maroni, self-proclaimed Sausage King, assures his customers that he's not making health food, these "haut dogs" are all-natural, preservative-free, and boast fancy flavorings such as cilantro, orange, fig, and apple. Only vegetarians will leave disappointed. *2011 Ocean Front Walk (north of Venice Blvd.).* 📞 310/822-5639. www.jodymaroni.com. $.

7 **Muscle Beach.** The famous outdoor gym originally resided just south of the Santa Monica Pier from the 1930s through the 1950s. Fitness gurus like Jack La Lanne and Joe Gold worked out here, as well as celebrities like Clark Gable, Kirk Douglas, and Jayne Mansfield. Later the gym migrated to facilities in Venice, where

Don't miss out on the delicious dogs at Jody Maroni's.

Look out for exploding biceps and more at Muscle Beach.

a young Arnold Schwarzenegger would stop in to pump up. Today the gym is still going strong. *Ocean Front Walk (2 blocks north of Venice Blvd.).*

8 **Venice Art Walls.** These walls are the only remnants of "The Pit," an area popular with graffiti artists from 1961 to 1999. Today a permit is required to paint on the walls (weekends only). The goal is to nurture high-quality street art while minimizing the vandalism sometimes associated with it. *Ocean Front Walk (btwn Windward & Market sts.).* www.veniceartwalls.com.

9 **Venice Murals by Rip Cronk.** Venice loves its street murals. Some of the most memorable ones were created in the late '80s and early '90s by an artist named Rip Cronk. Look for the following: "Morning Shot" (at Speedway and 18th Ct.), which features a towering Jim Morrison; "Venice Reconstituted" (25 Windward at Speedway), a loose interpretation of Botticelli's "The Birth of Venus;" and "Homage to a Starry Night," Cronk's nod to van Gogh (Wavecrest Ave. and Ocean).

Graffiti artists are welcome to display their best at the Venice Art Walls.

Head north on Ocean Front Walk, then east on Westminster Ave., and then go left at Abbot Kinney Blvd.

⑩ Abbot Kinney. Compared to the sea of humanity on the boardwalk, this stretch of funky-chic shops and small cafes is refreshingly laid-back. But if you see something you gotta have, you better grab it— these stores specialize in the hard-to-find and one-of-a-kind. After a good retail spree, peruse the books, art, and books about art at Equator Books (1103 Abbot Kinney Blvd.), a sunlit space that welcomes you off the street.

⑪ Jin Patisserie. Relax in the tranquil garden of this Asian-influenced cafe. An afternoon tea offers French teas, finger sandwiches, scones (yes, with clotted cream), cookies, and cakes—all made fresh

in the store. Many folks claim that the chocolate truffles are the best in the city. *1202 Abbot Kinney Blvd., Venice.* ☎ *310/399-8801. www. jinpatisserie.com. Tues–Sun 10:30am–7pm. $.*

Treat yourself to macaroon cakes and other delights at Jin Patisserie.

Culver City

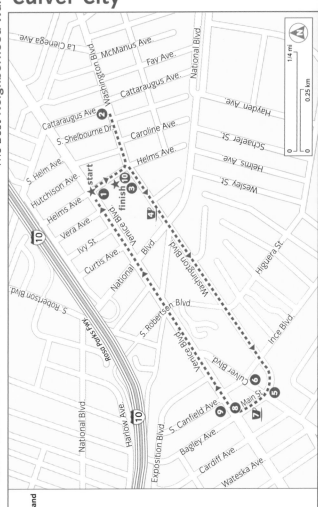

1 H.D. Buttercup
2 Museum of Design Art and Architecture (MODAA)
3 Last Chance Boutique
4 Café Surfas
5 Culver City Hotel
6 Culver Studios
7 BottleRock
8 Massage Garage
9 Museum of Jurassic Technology
10 Jazz Bakery

The "Heart of Screenland," as Culver City likes to call itself, may never again be responsible for more than half of America's motion picture production, as it was in the '30s and '40s during the golden age of MGM Studios. But the area has undergone a different kind of renaissance in recent years, with an influx of top-tier restaurants and cutting-edge art galleries.

① H.D. Buttercup. A 100,000-square-foot showcase of high-end furniture and arty home decor, this "manutailer" occupies the Art Deco building once home to the historic Helms Bakery (official bread supplier to the 1932 Olympics in Los Angeles). With more than 50 vendors offering an array of styles—Asian antique, country farmhouse, sleek contemporary, midcentury kitsch—you're bound to find something for your home sweet home. I love eyeballing the vintage steel furniture from Twenty Gauge. *3225 Helms Ave., at Washington Ave.* ☎ *310/558-8900. www.hdbuttercup.com. Mon–Sat 10am–7pm, Sun 11am–6pm.*

Head east along Washington Blvd.

② Museum of Design Art and Architecture (MODAA). Housing a gallery that explores the

Home-decorating choices are practically endless at H.D. Buttercup.

relationship between art and architecture, the MODAA building plays with your perceptions, like a digital image that's been manipulated into boxy fragments. For the past few years, MODAA has anchored the Culver City Art Walk, which includes a couple dozen galleries, most of which are clustered near the intersection of Washington and La Cienega boulevards. *8609 Washington Blvd.* ☎ *310/ 558-0902. www.modaagallery.com. Mon–Fri noon–6pm.*

Head back west along Washington Blvd.

③ Last Chance Boutique. The pitch is simple but deadly: designer clothes at discount prices. Gobble up labels like Chloe, Diane Von Furstenberg, Catherine Malandrino, and Vivienne Westwood at 50% to 80% off last season's retail prices. *8712 Washington Blvd.* ☎ *310/287-2333. www.shoplastchance.com. Mon–Fri 10am–6pm, Sat 10am–5pm.*

④ Café Surfas. Friendly, family-owned Surfas has long been a destination for gourmet ingredients and professional culinary tools; their cafe makes a perfect pit stop if your energy starts to flag. The breakfast panini are delish, but nothing beats the lavender lemon bars. *8777 Washington Blvd.* ☎ *310/558-1458. $.*

⑤ Culver City Hotel. Erected by Harry Culver in 1924, this pie wedge of a hotel is the most historic building in Culver City. During

the production heyday of MGM Studios, the hotel accommodated a steady stream of celebrity residents: Clark Gable, Greta Garbo, Joan Crawford, Buster Keaton, the Rat Pack, and Ronald Reagan. When *The Wizard of Oz* shot around the corner in 1939, more than 100 of the "munchkins" stayed here for 4 chaotic weeks; stories of their shenanigans later inspired the Chevy Chase film *Under the Rainbow*. The lobby's piano bar, Duke's Hideaway, honors its former owner, John Wayne. *9400 Culver Blvd.* ☎ *310/838-7963. www.culverhotel.com.*

Head next door, east on Washington Blvd.

❻ Culver Studios. The studio with the grand Colonial facade debuted in 1919, and it's been making history ever since. Films shot here include the original *King Kong* with Fay Wray; *Citizen Kane*, often

cited as cinema's highest achievement; Hitchcock films such as *Rebecca, Notorious,* and *Spellbound;* and perhaps most impressively, considering the scope of its scenes of Atlanta burning, *Gone With the Wind.* Over the years, the back lots have also bustled with television productions such as *The Andy Griffith Show, Lassie, Batman, Mad About You,* and *Arrested Development. 9336 W. Washington Blvd.*

Cross over Culver Blvd. to Main St.

❼ BottleRock. Offering a sophisticated selection (more than 800 bottles) in a breezy, unpretentious setting, this wine bar makes it easy to find a glass to fit your mood or food—they also serve cheese, charcuterie, and chocolates. *3847 Main St. (btwn Culver and Venice blvds.).* ☎ *310/836-9463. $.*

The historic Culver City Hotel.

Citizen Kane and the original *King Kong, among countless other classic films, were shot at Culver Studios.*

⑧ Massage Garage. They may drive the "spa as automobile tune-up shop" metaphor into the ground, but who cares? An hour-long massage is $45, about half of what some chi-chi spas in town charge. Facials are also available. *3812 Main St. ☎ 310/202-0082. www.themassagegarage.com.*

Head north to Venice Blvd. and go right.

⑨ ★ Museum of Jurassic Technology. You start with the non-sequitur name, and become more baffled the deeper you delve into the museum's intricacies—which is precisely what creator/curator David Wilson wants. A 2001 recipient of a McArthur "genius grant," Wilson promotes confusion as "a vehicle to open people's minds." If this sounds like gobbledygook, wait until you see the "Micro-miniatures" exhibit, featuring a sculpture of Pope John Paul II placed within the eye of a needle. *9341 Venice Blvd. ☎ 310/836-6131. www.mjt.org. Thurs 2–8pm, Fri–Sun noon–6pm. Suggested donation: $5 adults, $3 seniors & visitors 12–21, free for children under 12.*

⑩ Jazz Bakery. Check the schedule at this no-frills, not-for-profit venue, which presents live jazz 7 nights a week. Names like Charlie Byrd, Diana Krall, and Branford Marsalis have graced what *L.A. Weekly* calls "the most prestigious jazz space in Los Angeles." *3233 Helms Ave., at Venice Blvd. ☎ 310/271-9039. www.jazzbakery.com.*

L.A.'s most esteemed jazz venue, Jazz Bakery.

Silver Lake

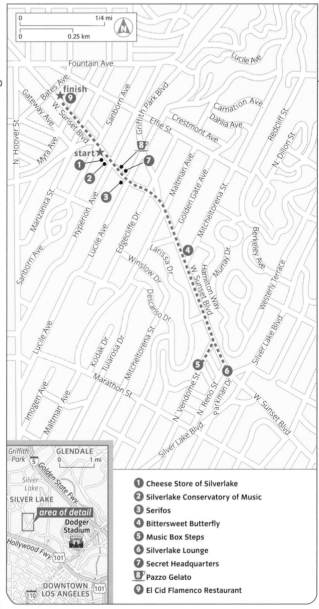

1. Cheese Store of Silverlake
2. Silverlake Conservatory of Music
3. Serifos
4. Bittersweet Butterfly
5. Music Box Steps
6. Silverlake Lounge
7. Secret Headquarters
8. Pazzo Gelato
9. El Cid Flamenco Restaurant

Silver Lake is a bohemian enclave east of Hollywood. Once home to the first movie studios (Mack Sennett, Vitagraph, and Walt Disney) and later the modernist architects (Neutra, Schindler), this hipster haven now offers one-of-a-kind shopping, eclectic eats, and a music scene that has arguably become a brand name. You can't see all of Silver Lake on foot, but the Sunset Junction (at Sunset and Santa Monica blvds.) makes for a happening hub.

1 Cheese Store of Silverlake.

At this quaint shop, you can grab all the fixings for a gourmet picnic: artisanal cheeses, hard-to-find wines, cured meats, and chocolates. *3926 W. Sunset Blvd. ☎ 323/644-7511. www.cheesestoresl.com. Mon 10am–6pm, Tues–Sat 10am–6:45pm, Sun 11am–5pm.*

2 Silverlake Conservatory of Music.

It's only fitting that Silver Lake, with its thriving indie music scene, would have its own school of rock. Flea, local music hero and bassist for the Red Hot Chili Peppers, founded the not-for-profit organization, which offers affordable lessons on singing and a variety of musical instruments to kids and adults. *3920 W. Sunset Blvd. ☎ 323/665-3363. www.silverlakeconservatory.com. Fri noon–9pm, Sat 10am–6pm.*

A customer checks out the goods at Serifos.

The Cheese Store of Silverlake is a gourmand's paradise.

3 Serifos.

This popular shop offers "gifts for everyone including yourself." Rummage through paint-by-number kits, classic movie stills, handmade jewelry, cool stationery, and stylin' baby clothes. *3814 W. Sunset Blvd. ☎ 323/660-7467. Mon & Wed–Fri 11am–7pm, Sat–Sun 10am–6pm.*

Head to the northeast corner of Sunset Blvd. and Micheltorena St.

4 Bittersweet Butterfly.

Gentlemen, if you're looking to get out of trouble with your lady (or perhaps into some trouble), try this cute boutique chock-full of fresh-cut flowers and high-end lingerie. *1406*

Flowers, lingerie, and more at Bittersweet Butterfly.

Micheltorena St. 📞 *323/660-4303.* *www.bittersweetbutterfly.com. Mon–Sat noon–8pm, Sun noon–5pm.*

Head a few blocks southeast on Sunset Blvd., and then go right at Vendome St.

5 Music Box Steps. Laurel and Hardy fans might enjoy a small detour to see where the comedic duo shot their 1932 Oscar®-winning short, *The Music Box,* in which Stan and Ollie had to deliver a piano up this ludicrously long stairway. *Btwn 923 & 925 Vendome St.*

Return to Sunset Blvd. and head right.

6 Silverlake Lounge. A funky hole-in-the-wall with a cash-only bar, this neighborhood favorite segues from up-and-coming bands on weekday nights to drag-queens on weekends without ever skipping a beat. *2906 Sunset Blvd.* 📞 *323/663-9636. Daily 5pm–2am.*

7 Secret Headquarters. Nurture your inner geek at this comic shop, which is so welcoming and well-designed you'd almost think that comic books were socially respectable for adults. *3817 W.*

Sunset Blvd. 📞 *323/666-2228. www. thesecretheadquarters.com. Mon–Sat 11am–9pm, Sun noon–7pm.*

8 Pazzo Gelato. Cold treats face fierce competition in Los Angeles, but this gelato and espresso bar recently earned "Best of L.A." from the *L.A. Weekly.* Pazzo Gelato prides itself on its daring flavors (chocolate coconut curry, green tea with ginger), so put those sample spoons to good use. *3827 W. Sunset Blvd.* 📞 *323/662-1410. www.pazzogelato.net. $.*

9 El Cid Flamenco Restaurant. On the site where D. W. Griffith screened his controversial epic *The Birth of a Nation* in 1915, this dinner-and-a-show club—modeled after a 16th-century Spanish tavern—serves up offbeat entertainment with a wink: flamenco dancing, burlesque, underground sketch comedy, and the occasional magician or fez-topped accordionist. *4212 W. Sunset Blvd.* 📞 *323/668-0318. www.elcidla.com. Mon–Tues 8pm–midnight, Wed–Sat 4pm–2am, Sun 11am–midnight.* ●

Tantalizing treats at Pazzo Gelato.

Shopping Best Bets

Hippest Store for Guys & Gals
★ American Rag Cie, *150 S. La Brea Ave. (p 77)*

Best **Music Store**
★★★ Amoeba Music, *6400 Sunset Blvd. (p 81)*

Best **Cheese Shop**
★★ Beverly Hills Cheese Shop, *419 N. Beverly Dr. (p 81)*

Best **Bookstore**
★★ Book Soup, *8818 Sunset Blvd. (p 75)*

Best **Chocolate Shop**
★ Boule, *420 N. La Cienega Blvd. (p 82)*

Best **Shopping for Tiny Dogs**
★ Fifi & Romeo Boutique, *7282 Beverly Blvd. (p 79)*

Best **Old-World Charm**
★ Santa Maria Novella, *8411 Melrose Place (p 79)*

Biggest **Scene**
★ Fred Segal, *8100 Melrose Ave. (p 77)*

Best **Kids' Clothing Store**
★★ La La Ling, *1810 N. Vermont Ave. (p 80)*

Best **Funky Gift Shop**
★ OK, *8303 W. Third St. (p 79)*

Best **Men's Boutique**
★★ Lisa Kline for Men, *143 S. Robertson Blvd. (p 78)*

Most **Puzzling**
★★ Puzzle Zoo, *1413 Third St. Promenade (p 80)*

Best **"New" Vintage Shoes**
★ Re-Mix, *7605½ Beverly Blvd. (p 78)*

Best **Kids Bookstore**
★★ Storyopolis, *12348 Ventura Blvd. (p 75)*

Best **Women's Shoes**
★★★ Neiman Marcus, *9700 Wilshire Blvd. (p 76);* and ★★ Sigerson Morrison, *8307 W. Third St. (p 78)*

Best Place to **Find a Party Dress in a Jiffy**
★ Betsey Johnson, *8050 Melrose Ave. (p 77)*

Best **Toy Store**
★★ Tom's Toys, *437 N. Beverly Dr. (p 80)*

Best **Wine Store**
★★ Wally's Wines, *2107 Westwood Blvd. (p 82)*

Rodeo Drive street sign.

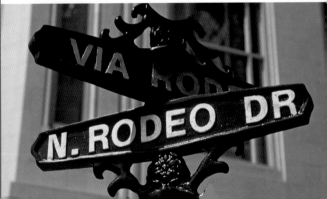

Santa Monica & the Beaches

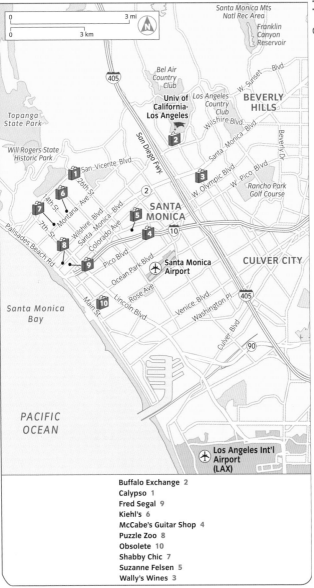

Buffalo Exchange 2
Calypso 1
Fred Segal 9
Kiehl's 6
McCabe's Guitar Shop 4
Puzzle Zoo 8
Obsolete 10
Shabby Chic 7
Suzanne Felsen 5
Wally's Wines 3

P 69: Fashion is girly and fun at Betsey Johnson.

Beverly Hills & the Westside

Agent Provocateur 13
arp 22
Barneys New York 33
Betsey Johnson 12
Beverly Hills Cheese Shop 31
Book Soup 1
Boule 14
Calypso 3
Decades 10
Diavolina 15
Edelweiss Chocolates 29
Erica Courtney 16
Ethel 25
Filly 27
Flight 001 26
Fred Segal 11
H.D. Buttercup 35
Jay Wolf 5

Kiehl's 17
Lily et Cie 28
Lisa Kline 18
Lisa Kline for Men 19
Neiman Marcus 32
OK 24
Ole Henriksen 4
Oliver Peoples 2
Noodle Stories 21
Paper Bag Princess 34
Paul Smith 9
Polkadots and Moonbeams Vintage 20
Santa Maria Novella 7
Sigerson Morrison 23
Suzanne Felsen 8
Tom's Toys 30
Wanna Buy a Watch 6

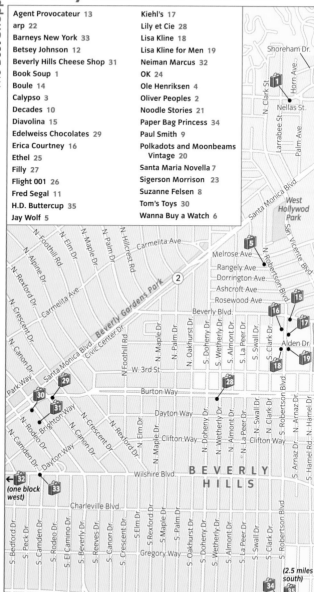

73

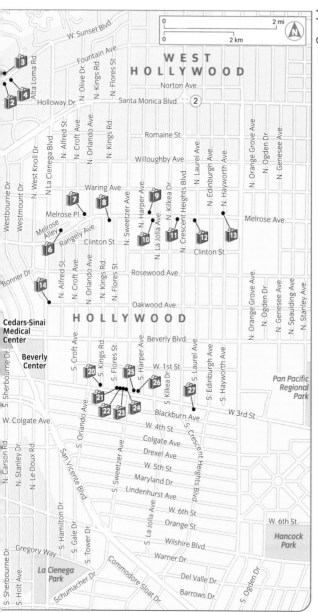

Hollywood, Los Feliz & Silver Lake

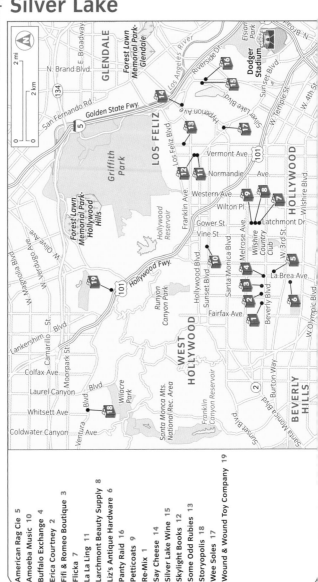

American Rag Cie 5
Amoeba Music 10
Buffalo Exchange 4
Erica Courtney 2
Fifi & Romeo Boutique 3
Flicka 7
La La Ling 11
Larchmont Beauty Supply 8
Liz's Antique Hardware 6
Panty Raid 16
Petticoats 9
Re-Mix 1
Say Cheese 14
Silver Lake Wine 15
Skylight Books 12
Some Odd Rubies 13
Storyopolis 18
Wee Soles 17
Wound & Wound Toy Company 19

Shopping A to Z

Beauty

★ **Kiehl's** ROBERTSON   Check out the deluxe beauty care products from this revered company, which first opened in NYC in 1851. *100 N. Robertson Blvd., at Alden Dr.* ☎ *310/860-0028. Also at 189 The Grove Dr., at Third & Fairfax aves.* ☎ *323/965-0569. And in Santa Monica at 1516 Montana Ave., at 15th St. www.kiehls. com. AE, DC, MC, V. Map p 72.*

Larchmont Beauty Supply

LARCHMONT   This may be the city's best collection of premium shampoos, soaps, candles, makeup, hair products, and more. *208 N. Larchmont Blvd. (btwn Third St. & Beverly Blvd.).* ☎ *323/461-0162. www. larchmontbeauty.com. AE, DISC, MC, V. Map p 74.*

★ **Ole Henriksen** WEST HOLLYWOOD   Luxurious facials and a superb line of skin-care products make this spa a hit among celebrities like Charlize Theron, Leonardo DiCaprio, and Mark Wahlberg. *8622 W. Sunset Blvd., west of Alta Loma Rd.* ☎ *310/854-7700. www.ole henriksen.com. AE, MC, V. Map p 72.*

Books

★★ **Book Soup** WEST HOLLYWOOD   The city's favorite independent bookstore has an amazing stock of books crammed into its nooks and crannies, a monstrous magazine rack, interesting clientele, and regular readings from visiting authors. *8818 Sunset Blvd., at Larabee St.* ☎ *310/659-3110. www. booksoup.com. AE, DISC, MC, V. Map p 72.*

★ **Skylight Books** LOS FELIZ   This independent bookstore specializes in literary fiction, film, and Los Angeles history. The staff recommendations are always intelligent and spot on. *1816½ N. Vermont Ave., at Melbourne Ave.* ☎ *323/666-2202. www.skylightbooks.com. AE, DISC, MC, V. Map p 74.*

★★ **Storyopolis** STUDIO CITY   Storyopolis, a children's bookstore, is best known for its story-time events and its Oprah-endorsed "Book Bushels," custom-made gift baskets of books. An art gallery with original art and limited-edition prints from top illustrators is also on site. *12348*

Whatever your beauty product needs, you're sure to find them at Larchmont Beauty Supply.

Fun vintage dresses adorn the windows at Polkadots and Moonbeams.

Ventura Blvd., at Laurel Grove Ave. ☎ 818/509-5600. www.storyopolis. com. AE, DISC, MC, V. Map p 74.

Department Stores

★★ Barneys New York BEVERLY HILLS   Fashion mavens navigate five luxurious floors of ready-to-wear from every designer on the planet. The women's shoes, bags, and beauty departments are especially alluring. Try the hoity-toity deli on the rooftop. *9570 Wilshire Blvd., at N. Camden Dr.* ☎ 310/276-4400. www. barneys.com. AE, MC, V. Map p 72.

★★★ Neiman Marcus BEVERLY HILLS   At this monument to retail escapism, a woman can rampage through the Manolo Blahniks in the highly regarded shoe department while her man waits patiently at the bar on the fourth floor. *9700 Wilshire Blvd. (btwn Santa Monica Blvd. & Brighton Way).* ☎ 310/550-5900. www.neimanmarcus.com. AE, MC, V. Map p 72.

Discount & Vintage

Buffalo Exchange HOLLYWOOD   Scour this secondhand store for designer labels, ironic T-shirts, and one-of-a-kind finds. *131 N. La Brea Ave., at First St.* ☎ 323/938-8604. *Also in Westwood at 10914 Kinross Ave., west of Westwood Blvd.* ☎ 310/208-7403. *And in Sherman Oaks at 14621 Ventura Blvd., west of Van Nuys Blvd.* ☎ 818/783-3420. www.buffaloexchange.com. MC, V. Map p 71.

★ Decades HOLLYWOOD   Stylists to the stars patrol the racks here for vintage couture from Hermès, Gucci, and YSL. *8214½ Melrose Ave., at Harper Ave.* ☎ 323/655-1960. www. decadesinc.com. AE, DISC, MC, V. Map p 72.

Lily et Cie BEVERLY HILLS   For Oscar®-night fashion, stars like Jennifer Lopez and Renee Zellweger know to go to Rita Watnick's store for vintage gowns from Givenchy, Chanel, and more. *9044 Burton Way, at Doheny Dr.* ☎ 310/724-5757. www.lilyetcie.com. AE, DISC, MC, V. Map p 72.

Paper Bag Princess BEVERLY HILLS   This store feels like a museum of vintage designer wear, but the service can be snooty. *8818 Olympic Blvd., at Robertson Blvd.* ☎ 310/385-9036. www.thepaper bagprincess.com. AE, MC, V. Map p 72.

★ Polkadots and Moonbeams Vintage

WEST HOLLYWOOD This girly-girl shop is the perfect place to find vintage cocktail dresses. A few doors down is a sister store specializing in contemporary party wear. *8367 W. Third St., at S. Kings Rd.* ☎ *323/651-1746. www.polkadots andmoonbeams.com. AE, MC, V. Map p 72.*

Fashion

★ American Rag Cie

HOLLYWOOD This popular store features up-and-coming designers, well-selected vintage wear, retro sneakers, a massive denim selection, and hip accessories—all guaranteed to make you cooler. *150 S. La Brea Ave. (btwn W. First & W. Second sts.).* ☎ *323/935-3154. www.american ragcie.co.jp. AE, MC, V. Map p 74.*

★ Betsey Johnson

WEST HOLLYWOOD If you're looking for a sexy little number to wear to a party, check out the colorful bouquet of playful, vintage-inspired dresses. *8050 Melrose Ave., at N. Laurel Ave.* ☎ *323/852-1534. www.betsey johnson.com. AE, MC, V. Map p 72.*

★ Calypso

WEST HOLLYWOOD Christiane Celle's elegant, French-inspired designs are comfortable

Treat yourself to a pair of stylish, sexy shoes from Diavolina.

The landmark Fred Segal clothing store.

and flowing, perfect for warm SoCal weather. *8635 W. Sunset Blvd., at Sunset Plaza Dr.* ☎ *310/652-4454. Also in Santa Monica at 225 26th St., at San Vicente Blvd.* ☎ *310/ 434-9601. www.calypso-celle.com. AE, MC, V. Map p 72.*

Diavolina

BEVERLY HILLS For footwear that'll get you noticed, check out this huge selection of shoes from designers like Chloe and Marc Jacobs. *156 N. Robertson Blvd. (btwn Alden Dr. & Beverly Blvd.).* ☎ *310/550-1341. AE, MC, V. Map p 72.*

Ethel

WEST HOLLYWOOD This small store leans more toward stylish, well-made basics than flashy trends, and prices tend to be reasonable. *8235½ W. Third St., at S. Harper Ave.* ☎ *323/658-8602. AE, MC, V. Map p 72.*

★ Filly

WEST HOLLYWOOD Mosey into this country-chic boutique stocked with hip, urban designers. *8032 W. Third St., at S. Laurel Ave.* ☎ *323/653-7200. www.fillyfilly.com. AE, MC, V. Map p 72.*

★ Fred Segal

WEST HOLLYWOOD No clothing store draws more celebrity shoppers than this landmark. The only thing reasonably priced is the parking, which is free. *8100 Melrose Ave., at Crescent Heights Blvd.* ☎ *323/651-4129. Also in Santa Monica at 500 Broadway, at*

Fifth St. ☎ 310/394-9814. www. fredsegalfun.com. AE, MC, V. Maps p 71 and p 72.

★ **Jay Wolf** BEVERLY HILLS   Ask a stylish, successful L.A. man where he got that impeccable-looking shirt, and he may very well say Jay Wolf. And then he might add "But don't tell everybody! It's a hidden gem!" Right. 517 N. Robertson Blvd., at Rangely Ave. ☎ 310/273-9893. Map p 72.

★ **Lisa Kline** BEVERLY HILLS Pretty young things swarm this shop for its form-fitting fashions, also a favorite among celebrities like Jessica Biel and Eva Longoria. 136 S. Robertson Blvd., at Alden Dr. ☎ 310/246-0907. www.lisakline.com. AE, MC, V. Map p 72.

★★ **Lisa Kline for Men** BEVERLY HILLS   Men going for that L.A. look shop here for the "right" kind of shirts, jeans, and jackets. The decor features boxing gloves and catcher's mitts, reminding fellas that shopping is indeed a manly pursuit. 143 S. Robertson Blvd., at Alden Dr. ☎ 310/385-7113. www.lisakline.com. AE, MC, V. Map p 72.

★ **Noodle Stories** WEST HOLLY-WOOD   This collection of women's clothing emphasizes subtlety, simplicity, and sophistication. Designers include Comme des Garçons, Martin Margiela, and Yohji Yamamoto. 8323 W. Third St., at N. Flores St. ☎ 323/651-1782. AE, MC, V. Map p 72.

Oliver Peoples WEST HOLLY-WOOD   This fashionable optical shop sells top-quality shades and frames for stars (Jack Nicholson, Gwen Stefani) or folks that just want to look (and see) like them. 8642 W. Sunset Blvd., at Sunset Plaza Dr. ☎ 310/657-2553. www.oliverpeoples. com. AE, MC, V. Map p 72.

★★ **Paul Smith** WEST HOLLYWOOD Designer Paul Smith is celebrated for his snappy, British style, and his slightly mod shirts and suits will make any man look like a million bucks. 8221 Melrose Ave., at N. La Jolla Ave. ☎ 323/951-4800. www. paulsmith.co.uk. AE, DC, DISC, MC, V. Map p 72.

★ **Re-Mix** WEST HOLLYWOOD Vintage, but not worn. "Say what?" you say. Most of these shoes—old-schoolers like wingtips, babydolls, and saddle shoes—come from dead stock, or have been reproduced to match the vintage style. 7605½ Beverly Blvd., at N. Curson Ave. ☎ 323/936-6210. www.remixvintageshoes. com. AE, DISC, MC, V. Map p 74.

★★ **Sigerson Morrison** WEST HOLLYWOOD   This NYC export showcases sleek bags, shoes, and boots, and their sexy flat sandals have inspired a passionate legion of fans. 8307 W. Third St., at S. Sweetzer Ave. ☎ 323/655-6133. www. sigersonmorrison.com. AE, DISC, MC, V. Map p 72.

Some Odd Rubies LOS FELIZ This cozy boutique, with a sister shop on NYC's Lower Eastside, sells vintage pieces which have been stylishly reworked. 1937 Hillhurst Ave., at Franklin Ave. ☎ 323/644-9088. www.someoddrubies.com. AE, MC, V. Map p 74.

In addition to stylish fashions, jewelry and accessories are sold at Some Odd Rubies.

Gifts

★ **Fifi & Romeo Boutique** WEST HOLLYWOOD This luxury boutique for little pooches offers cashmere and angora sweaters, faux fur-trimmed coats, jewel-encrusted collars, and that sense of validation that tiny canines sometimes need. *7282 Beverly Blvd., at N. Poinsettia Place.* ☎ *323/857-7214. www.fifiand romeo.com. AE, MC, V. Map p 74.*

Flight 001 WEST HOLLYWOOD Take a trip here for the coolest retro-style travel gear and accessories: eyeshades, toiletry bags, stylish luggage tags, and electrical adapters. *8235 W. Third St., at S. Harper Ave.* ☎ *323/966-0001. www.flight001. com. AE, MC, V. Map p 72.*

★ **OK** WEST HOLLYWOOD Blown-glass vases, antique phones, obscure art books, and funky lamps—unusual gift ideas abound at this gallery-like store. *8303 W. Third St., at S. Sweetzer Ave.* ☎ *323/653-3501. www.ok store.la. AE, MC, V. Map p 72.*

★ **Santa Maria Novella** WEST HOLLYWOOD On Melrose Place, take a side trip to Florence, Italy. This boutique carries soaps, lotions, and scents based upon the same recipes used 400 years ago by the Dominican friars of Santa Maria Novella. *8411 Melrose Place, at N. Orlando Ave.* ☎ *323/651-3754. www. smnovella.it. AE, MC, V. Map p 72.*

Home Decor

H.D. Buttercup CULVER CITY This "manutailer" fills 150,000 square feet with more than 50 individual vendors of quality furniture and furnishings. *3225 Helms Ave., at Washington Ave.* ☎ *310/558-8900. www.hdbuttercup.com. AE, DISC, MC, V. Map p 72.*

Liz's Antique Hardware HOLLYWOOD This store specializes in door, window, and furniture hardware from 1860 to 1970, as well as

This wooden girl model is one of the obscure and somewhat unsettling objects that can be found at Obsolete.

vintage and contemporary lighting fixtures. *453 S. La Brea Ave. (btwn W. Fourth & W. Sixth sts.).* ☎ *323/ 939-4403. www.lahardware.com. AE, MC, V. Map p 74.*

★ **Obsolete** SANTA MONICA This art store/gallery carries vaguely melancholic and creepy pieces like antique models of the human brain, and sculptures with found objects like baby doll heads. *222 Main St., (btwn Rose Ave. & Marine St.).* ☎ *310/399-0024. www.obsolete inc.com. AE, MC, V. Map p 71.*

Shabby Chic SANTA MONICA English lass Rachel Ashwell brings her cozy and relaxed line of linens and furniture to Santa Monica. *1013 Montana Ave., at 10th St.* ☎ *310/ 394-1975. www.shabbychic.com. AE, MC, V. Map p 71.*

Jewelry

arp WEST HOLLYWOOD This handsome jewelry store carries the organic, almost minimalist designs of Ted Muehling. *8311½ W. Third St., at Sweetzer Ave.* ☎ *323/653-7764. AE, MC, V. Map p 72.*

Erica Courtney WEST HOLLY-WOOD   Many an A-list lovely, such as Julia Roberts or Jessica Alba, has paraded these timeless designs down the red carpet. *7465 Beverly Blvd., at Gardner St.* ☎ *323/938-2373. Also in Beverly Hills at 117 N. Robertson Blvd., at Alden Dr.* ☎ *310/858-6700. www.ericacourtney.com. AE, MC, V. Map p 72.*

Suzanne Felsen WEST HOLLY-WOOD   Giving unusual stones a modern twist, this designer is one of L.A.'s most popular. *8332 Melrose Ave., at N. Kings Rd.* ☎ *323/653-5400. Also in Santa Monica at 2525 Michigan Ave.* ☎ *310/315-1972. www.suzannefelsen.com. AE, MC, V. Maps p 71 and p 72.*

Wanna Buy a Watch WEST HOL-LYWOOD   Take the time to check out this shop's selection of high-end vintage watches like Rolex, Patek Philippe, and Cartier. *8465 Melrose Ave., at La Cienega Blvd.* ☎ *323/653-0467. www.wannabuyawatch.com. AE, DISC, MC, V. Map p 72.*

Kids

★ **Flicka** LARCHMONT   The clothes for infants and toddlers are sweet, trendy, and well-made. Finding the perfect baby shower or birthday gift is a snap, and the free wrapping helps. *204 N. Larchmont Blvd. (btwn Beverly Blvd. & First St.).* ☎ *323/466-5822. AE, MC, V. Map p 74.*

★★ **La La Ling** LOS FELIZ   If your kid simply has to have what Maddox Jolie-Pitt is wearing this season, hit this funky shop stocked with designer duds for little folks. *1810 N. Vermont Ave., at Melbourne Ave.* ☎ *323/664-4400. www.lalaling.com. MC, V. Map p 74.*

★★ **Puzzle Zoo** SANTA MONICA   Conveniently located on Third Street Promenade, this lively toy store specializes in puzzles (naturally) as well

Find the perfect gift for the baby or toddler in your life at Flicka.

as licensed toys, such as action figures from *Star Wars, Lord of the Rings,* and *Austin Powers. 1413 Third St. Promenade, at Arizona Ave.* ☎ *310/393-9201. www.puzzlezoo. com. AE, DISC, MC, V. Map p 71.*

★★ **Tom's Toys** BEVERLY HILLS   As much for nostalgic adults as for children, this large, independent toy store carries the classics—Lincoln Logs, Tinker Toys, Rock 'Em Sock 'Em Robots—as well as new faves like Thomas the Tank Engine. *437 N. Beverly Dr., at Santa Monica Blvd.* ☎ *310/247-9822. AE, DISC, MC, V. Map p 72.*

Wee Soles SILVER LAKE   Where hip parents go to buy hip shoes for their hip kids. *3827 W. Sunset Blvd., Suite E (at Lucile Ave.).* ☎ *323/667-0774. AE, MC, V. Map p 74.*

Wound & Wound Toy Company UNIVERSAL CITY   This shop is stuffed with windup robots, tin collectibles, music boxes, novelty action figures, and every windup toy you could imagine. *1000 Universal Studios Blvd., at Universal City Place.* ☎ *818/509-8129. www.thewound andwound.com. MC, V. Map p 74.*

Lingerie

Agent Provocateur WEST HOL-LYWOOD   The grande dame of Los Angeles lingerie, this sexy boutique sells high-end lingerie with matching price tags. You'll love the service you get from the ladies dressed in matching frocks. *7961 Melrose Ave., at N. Hayworth Ave.* ☎ *323/653-0229. www.agentprovocateur.com. AE, MC, V. Map p 72.*

Panty Raid SILVER LAKE   Eastside hipsters shop here for its fun variety of frilly underthings from designers like Hanky Panky, Mary Green, and Cosabella. *2378½ Glendale Blvd., at Brier Ave.* ☎ *323/668-1888. www. pantyraidshop.com. AE, DISC, MC, V. Map p 74.*

Petticoats LARCHMONT   This shop offers a cutesy selection of women's lingerie, PJs, robes, and other pretty things. *115 Larchmont Blvd., at W First St.* ☎ *323/467-7178. www.petticoatslingerie.com. AE, DISC, MC, V. Map p 74.*

Music & Musical Instruments
★★★ **Amoeba Music** HOLLY-WOOD   In the war of music retailers,

For fun and frilly lingerie, head to Panty Raid in Silver Lake.

The Beverly Hills Cheese Shop offers cheese, cheese, and more delicious cheese.

score one for the little guy—and by "little," I mean *huuuge* but independently owned. The extra-large music store's staff, walking encyclopedias of music, don't mind you asking, "What's the name of that band . . . with that song; it kinda goes like . . . ?" *6400 Sunset Blvd., at Ivar Ave.* ☎ *323/245-6400. www.amoeba.com. DISC, MC, V. Map p 74.*

McCabe's Guitar Shop SANTA MONICA   This homey shop sports the largest selection of stringed instruments in the state, and often hosts acoustic sets from performers like Beck, Bonne "Prince" Billy, and Peter Case. *3101 Pico Blvd., at 31st St.* ☎ *310/828-4497. www.mccabes. com. AE, DISC, MC, V. Map p 71.*

Specialty Foods & Wines
★★ **Beverly Hills Cheese Shop** BEVERLY HILLS   Since 1967 cheese-lovers have flocked here for a staggering selection of heavenly cheeses, more than 500 varieties from around the globe. *419 N. Beverly Dr., at Brighton Way.* ☎ *310/278-2855. www.cheesestorebh.com. AE, DC, DISC, MC, V. Map p 72.*

Silver Lake Wines has something for you, no matter what your budget.

★ **Boule** WEST HOLLYWOOD   The artful chocolates and European-style pastries (especially the macaroons) make great gifts, stylishly presented in beribboned, light-blue boxes. *420 N. La Cienega Blvd., at Oakwood Ave.* ☎ *310/289-9977. www.boulela.com. AE, MC, V. Map p 72.*

Edelweiss Chocolates BEVERLY HILLS   The old-fashioned chocolate shop, a Beverly Hills landmark since 1942, stays fresh by creating all their delectables on the premises. Happy customers have included Katherine Hepburn, Lauren Bacall, and Steven Spielberg. The fudge rocks. *444 N. Canon Dr., at Burton Way.* ☎ *310/275-0341. www.edelweisschocolates.com. AE, MC, V. Map p 72.*

★ **Say Cheese** SILVER LAKE   Say yes to this adorable spot, which offers a spread of French cheeses and gourmet nibbles like olives and anchovies. An adjoining cafe puts the cheese to fine use on rich sandwiches such as brie-and-ham croissants. *2800 Hyperion Ave., at Rowena Ave.* ☎ *323/665-0545. AE, MC, V. Map p 74.*

★ **Silver Lake Wines** SILVER LAKE   This small shop focuses on top-notch, small-batch wines for all budgets. Sample a few at the relaxing tastings ($8–$12) offered on Monday and Thursday evenings. *2395 Glendale Blvd., at Brier Ave.* ☎ *323/662-9024. www.silverlakewines.com. AE, MC, V. Map p 74.*

★★ **Wally's Wines** WESTWOOD   Lovers of the grape know to hit this Westside warehouse for its vast selection and friendly, knowledgeable staff. Great gift baskets are also available. *2107 Westwood Blvd., at Mississippi Ave.* ☎ *310/475-0606. www.wallywine.com. AE, DISC, MC, V. Map p 71.* ●

L.A.'s **Best Beaches**

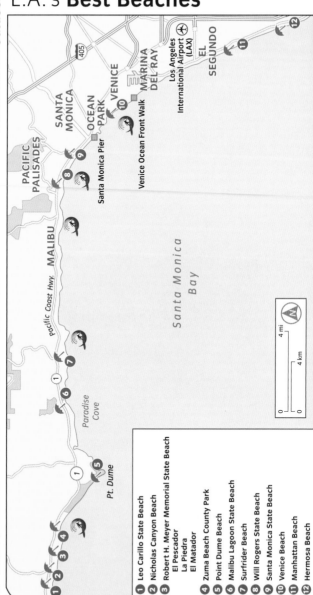

1. Leo Carillo State Beach
2. Nicholas Canyon Beach
3. Robert H. Meyer Memorial State Beach
   El Pescador
   La Piedra
   El Matador
4. Zuma Beach County Park
5. Point Dume Beach
6. Malibu Lagoon State Beach
7. Surfrider Beach
8. Will Rogers State Beach
9. Santa Monica State Beach
10. Venice Beach
11. Manhattan Beach
12. Hermosa Beach

Previous page: Picturesque Point Dume.

It's not *if* you're going to the beach, it's *when.* So when you do go, here's how you find the ones that are right for you. One glaringly obvious tip: Weekends are going to be much more crowded than other times, particularly if it's warm. And for God's sake, wear sunscreen. START: Malibu.

❶ Leo Carrillo State Beach.
Named after the actor who played Pancho, sidekick to the Cisco Kid in the 1950s television show, Leo Carrillo is a 1½-mile-wide sandy beach where Hollywood used to shoot surf flicks like *Gidget*. Kids love searching for hermit crabs in the tide pools and coastal caves. Family-friendly campgrounds are available; Wi-Fi is free for campers, and a Starbuck's is a short drive away. Aah, roughing it. *35000 W. Pacific Coast Hwy., Malibu.* ☎ *818/880-0350.*

❷ Nicholas Canyon Beach.
Called Zeroes by locals, this sandy spot is usually far less crowded than nearby beaches like Leo Carrillo or Zuma; perhaps the lack of a sign on the Pacific Coast Highway has something to do with it. It's certainly no secret to local surfers who dig the left point break on south swells. Families enjoy the easy access and picnic tables. *33850 W. Pacific Coast Hwy., Malibu.* ☎ *310/457-2525.*

❸ ★★ Robert H. Meyer Memorial State Beach (El

El Matador Beach.

Pescador, La Piedra, and El Matador). These three hidden coves are gems tucked against the Malibu cliffs. If you can manage your way down a short trail and/or rickety staircases, clean pockets of sand and alluring sea caves await you. Crowded summer weekends can kill

Windsurfers take advantage of a beautiful day at Leo Carrillo State Beach.

the magical vibe, but if you make it midweek or, better yet, off-season, you might be able stake out a patch of paradise. No lifeguard on duty. *32900, 32700 & 32350 W. Pacific Coast Hwy. (btwn Broad Beach & Decker Canyon rds.), Malibu.* ☎ *818/ 880-0350.*

④ ★ Zuma Beach County Park. This huge and hugely popular stretch of white, sandy beach has the proverbial "something for every-body": swimming, surfing, body-boarding, fishing, volleyball, snack bars, playground swings, restrooms, and plenty of parking. Weekends are a zoo, but weekdays are surprisingly tame. *30000 W. Pacific Coast Hwy. (btwn Kanan Dume & Encinal Canyon rds.), Malibu.* ☎ *310/457-9701.*

⑤ ★★ Point Dume Beach. Don't tell anybody, but this is my favorite beach in Los Angeles. The Point lies just south of Zuma, but it lacks Zuma's crowds (and, frankly, its amenities and activities, as well). Frolic in the surf, or hike up into the Point Dume State Preserve and take in the views (perfect for whale-watching during the Dec–Mar

migration season). From the sum-mit, you can descend to a smaller, isolated beach called Pirate's Cove. *7103 Westward Rd. (at the PCH), Malibu.* ☎ *310/457-9701.*

⑥ Malibu Lagoon State Beach. Malibu Creek meets the Pacific Ocean at this lagoon, and the wetlands create a unique bird sanc-tuary, a pit stop for more than 200 species during their annual migra-tions. Watch the birds, watch the surfers, go fishing on the Malibu Pier, or lounge on the beach. When you're ready to reengage your mind, pop into the Adamson House, renowned for its display of Malibu tiles; or try the Malibu Lagoon Museum, which traces the history of the area from the days of the Chumash Indians. *23200 Pacific Coast Hwy. (at Cross Creek Rd.), Malibu.* ☎ *818/880-0350.*

⑦ Surfrider Beach. Next to the Malibu Pier is this surfing hot spot, probably the most-surfed break in the county. Arguably the birthplace of surfing in California, Surfrider still enjoys a fine reputation for the consistency of its summer waves, although local surfers aren't fond of

Pelicans enjoy the sunshine at Malibu Lagoon State Beach.

sharing them with out-of-towners. *Part of Malibu Lagoon State Beach, 23200 Pacific Coast Hwy. (at Cross Creek Rd.), Malibu.* ☎ *818/880-0350.*

⑧ Will Rogers State Beach. The 3-mile-long beach provides playground and gymnastic equipment, plenty of new restrooms, volleyball courts (especially near Chautauqua Blvd.), and the start of the South Bay Bike Path that ends 22 miles south in Torrance County Beach. One downside: Although the surf looks gentle, pollution can be a factor, especially after a rain, when storm drains empty. *16000 Pacific Coast Hwy., Pacific Palisades.* ☎ *310/305-9503.*

⑨ Santa Monica State Beach. White sands, restrooms, easy access with ample parking, hot dogs, and in full view of the Santa Monica Pier—sheesh, how much more can you ask of a beach so close to all the action? While it may not be a "get there early and camp out all day" type beach, it's a great way to combine beach time with other activities. Again, rains can contribute to higher pollution levels in the water. *400–2900 blocks of Ocean Ave., Santa Monica.*

⑩ ★★ Venice Beach. Consider the beach to be a sandy extension of wild Venice Boardwalk. It's about entertainment, not relaxation—the sound of waves crashing isn't quite as soothing when accompanied by an impromptu drum circle. You may as well rent some skates or a bike, and join the streams heading up and down the boardwalk. *3100 Ocean Front Walk, Venice.* ☎ *310/399-2775.*

Volleyball is a major draw at Manhattan Beach.

⑪ Manhattan Beach. Surfing and volleyball are the two big draws on this big beach with small-town friendliness. More than 150 volleyball courts (for both pros and amateurs) dot the 2 miles of wide, flat beach. Surfers catch killer waves at El Porto at the north end of the beach. *Manhattan Beach Blvd. (at Highland Ave.), Manhattan Beach.*

⑫ ★ Hermosa Beach. Like its neighbor, Manhattan Beach, this beach community is proud of its surfing and volleyball. A few years ago, a Hermosa Beach Surfer's Hall of Fame was created on the pier to help support the town's claim as the birthplace of surfing in California. Pro volleyball tournaments are a regular feature and draw huge crowds. When the sun goes down, the bar scene on Pier Avenue heats up. *Hermosa Ave. (at 33rd St.), Hermosa Beach.* ☎ *310/372-4477.*

x

x

x

Hikes

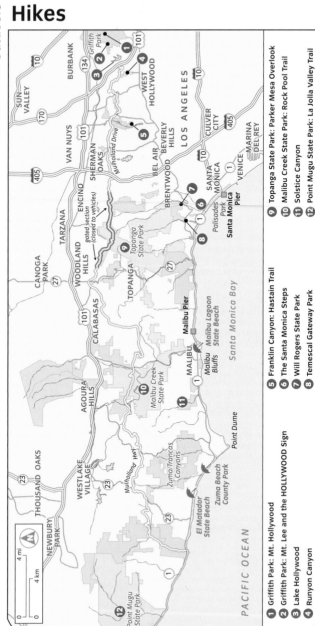

1 Griffith Park: Mt. Hollywood
2 Griffith Park: Mt. Lee and the HOLLYWOOD Sign
3 Lake Hollywood
4 Runyon Canyon
5 Franklin Canyon: Hastain Trail
6 The Santa Monica Steps
7 Will Rogers State Park
8 Temescal Gateway Park
9 Topanga State Park: Parker Mesa Overlook
10 Malibu Creek State Park: Rock Pool Trail
11 Solstice Canyon
12 Point Mugu State Park: La Jolla Valley Trail

Funny thing about folks in **Los Angeles**—they wrinkle their noses at the idea of walking a block to dinner, but call something a "hike," and it's a stampede of iPods and Nikes. Here are a few places to get out of the gritty city, or at least above it.

1 ★★★ **Griffith Park: Mount Hollywood.** A wide sandy trail takes you to the top of Mount Hollywood, undoubtedly the best view in all of Griffith Park. Being the most popular hike in the city's most popular park, it can get crowded. Take the Charlie Turner Trailhead, which begins across from the Griffith Observatory, for a 2.5-mile loop. For a 5-mile version, start at the Fern Dell Trail near the Fern Dell Nature Museum. *Griffith Observatory, 2800 E. Observatory Rd.* ☎ *213/473-0800. www.griffithobservatory.org. Ferndell Nature Museum: Ferndell Dr. (north of Los Feliz Blvd.).* ☎ *323/666-5046. Trails open daily 6am–dusk.*

2 ★★ **Griffith Park: Mt. Lee and the HOLLYWOOD Sign.** This is my favorite way to experience the sign, looking over the tops of the 45-foot-high letters at the city sprawled out below. Think about all the people who could be looking up at the HOLLYWOOD sign right now for

inspiration, and wave at them. *Take Beachwood Dr. north to Hollyridge Dr. Follow the Hollyridge Trail northeast. After a half-mile, take Mulholland Trail west. At Mount Lee Dr., head north & follow the trail to the back of the sign.*

3 **Lake Hollywood.** Okay, it's not exactly a hike, but the 3.2-mile path around the reservoir is flat and paved, ideal for jogging and walking. And you can't beat the scenery: The blue-green water shimmers, nearly secluded by the pines and sycamores; north in the hills, the HOLLYWOOD sign looms; south beyond Mulholland Dam, Hollywood settles in the distance. As you pass the lushly landscaped residences, look for the striped walls of Castillo del Lago, once the home of mobster Bugsy Siegel, and later of Madonna. *Lake Hollywood Dr.* ☎ *323/463-0830. Daily 6:30am–sunset. Take Barham Blvd. north to Lake Hollywood Dr.*

An aerial view of the scenic Lake Hollywood.

4 Runyon Canyon. An off-leash dog park just a bone's throw from Hollywood and Highland, the canyon's trails are always packed with people and their pooches. Make it to the highest point in the park, Indian Rock, and you'll earn a lovely panorama of Hollywood and beyond. Plus, there's something refreshing about spotting a celeb, baseball cap pulled low, dutifully picking up after his or her dog. *2000 N. Fuller Ave (at Hillside Ave.), Hollywood. ☎ 323/666-5046. Daily dawn–dusk.*

5 Franklin Canyon: Hastain Trail. Tucked away between the San Fernando Valley and Beverly Hills, these 605 chaparral-covered acres offer a lake (originally a reservoir built in 1914 by William Mulholland), a small duck pond, and 5 miles of hiking trails, the most popular being the pretty Hastain Trail, a hearty 2.3-mile workout. Grab a map near the park's entrance at the Sooky Goldman Nature Center. *2600 Franklin Canyon Dr. (at Mullholland Dr.), Beverly Hills. ☎ 310/858-7272. Head north on Beverly Dr., turn left on Coldwater/Beverly Dr. & turn left again on Beverly Dr. Go right at Franklin Canyon Dr.*

C'mon—a little exercise won't kill ya. Go for a hike in Runyon Canyon. Enjoy the views while you're at it.

Feel the burn on the Santa Monica steps.

6 The Santa Monica Steps. Enjoy hiking except for that pesky back-to-nature business? Here's a popular urban hike—actually more of a nightmarishly long set of stairs that will burn your legs and lungs. Locals come for an intense workout, with lovely views of the ocean—and of each other. Try the loop: Go up the concrete steps, jog a few hundred feet east on Adelaide Street, and come down the wooden steps. Repeat ad nauseam. *Fourth St. (btwn Adelaide St. & San Vicente Blvd.).*

7 ★ Will Rogers State Park. Good ol' Will Rogers left us his ranch, 186 acres at the western edge of the Santa Monica Mountains, to enjoy. A relatively easy hike lifts you into the countryside along the ranch's perimeter, where highlights include **Inspiration Point;** from here you can take in the gorgeous ocean and mountain views. *1501 Will Rogers Park Rd. (off Sunset Blvd.), Pacific Palisades. ☎ 310/454-8212. Daily 8am–sunset.*

8 ★★★ Temescal Gateway Park. The popular Canyon Loop follows a scenic ridgeline, then dips into a woodsy canyon, at the bottom of which is a small waterfall (don't get too excited—it barely trickles during the dry summer season). A steep climb out of the canyon yields expansive ocean views, and the adventurous can climb another half-mile up to Skull Rock, where the views are even better; both offer gentle ocean breezes to cool your brow. *15601 Sunset Blvd. (at Temescal Canyon Rd.), Pacific Palisades.* ☎ *310/454-1395. Daily sunrise–sunset.*

⑨ ★★★ **Topanga State Park: Parker Mesa Overlook.** The largest state park within the boundaries of a major city, Topanga is a whopper: 11,000 acres of grassland, live oak groves, and sandstone cliffs overlooking the Pacific Ocean. With 36 miles of trails (including some backbreakers that extend into the neighboring parks of Will Rogers and Point Mugu), you've got plenty of options. I recommend the hike from Trippet Ranch to the Parker Mesa Overlook, where you can absorb the stunning 360-degree views. *20825 Entrada Dr.* ☎ *310/455-2465. Daily 8am–sunset. From Pacific Coast Hwy., travel north on Topanga Canyon Blvd., and then turn right on Entrada Rd.*

⑩ ★ **Malibu Creek State Park: Rock Pool Trail.** Former owner Twentieth Century Fox fully exploited the park's "so close, yet so far away" quality, using it as a backdrop for movies *(Planet of the Apes, Tarzan)* and television shows *(M.A.S.H.).* An easy walk brings you to a refreshing Rock Pool, although it can get overcrowded on summer weekends. Try rock climbing along its volcanic rock walls. For a more serene water setting, head along the trail to Century Lake, set in a grove of redwoods. *M.A.S.H.* fans might want to trek further down Crags Road to visit "Korea," where a couple of rusty

The serene Rock Pool at Malibu Creek State Park.

jeeps appear to be the only casualties of the war. *1925 Las Virgenes Rd. (at Mulholland Dr.), Malibu.* ☎ *818/880-0367. Daily sunrise–sunset.*

⑪ ★ **Solstice Canyon.** For centuries, Chumash Indians used the beautiful coastal canyon for food and shelter, but a hike along the Solstice Canyon Trail will yield evidence of not-so-ancient ruins—an architecturally significant residence designed by the renowned Paul Williams burned down in 1982. The area, called Tropical Terrace, also features a lovely 30-foot waterfall and lush foliage. Play archaeologist, or simply sun on the large boulders in the creek. *Corral Canyon Rd. (at PCH), Malibu.* ☎ *805/370-2301. Daily 8am–sunset.*

⑫ ★★ **Point Mugu State Park: La Jolla Valley Trail.** A longer drive from Los Angeles than the other options, Point Mugu throws in plenty of incentives: 70 miles of hiking trails, 13,300 acres of state park, and miles of jagged coastline. The La Jolla Valley Trail cuts through rolling grasslands, lush canyons, and, in spring, blooming wildflowers and burbling waterfalls. The most dramatic vistas are along the oceanside hills on the way to Mugu Peak. *9000 W. Pacific Coast Hwy., Malibu.* ☎ *818/880-0350. Daily 7am–10pm.*

Griffith Park

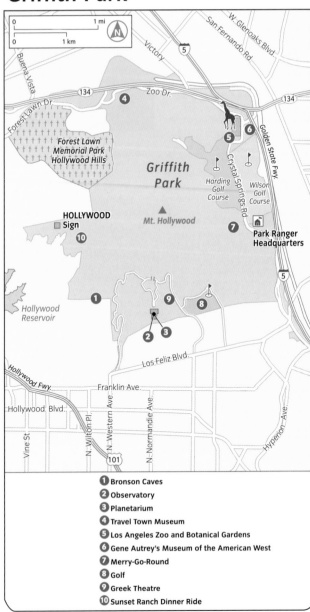

1 Bronson Caves
2 Observatory
3 Planetarium
4 Travel Town Museum
5 Los Angeles Zoo and Botanical Gardens
6 Gene Autrey's Museum of the American West
7 Merry-Go-Round
8 Golf
9 Greek Theatre
10 Sunset Ranch Dinner Ride

Welsh mining millionaire **Griffith J. Griffith** believed every great city needs a great park, and for Christmas in 1896, he gave to the people of Los Angeles 3,015 acres to create "a place of rest and relaxation for the masses, a resort for the rank and file." Today it is one of the largest urban parks in the United States and beloved by Angelenos. *Daily 6am–10pm.*

1 Bronson Caves. To the Batcave! The caves, actually short tunnels, are man-made, the result of quarry operations to gather crushed rock for paving Sunset Boulevard and other major roads. Most folks will recognize the caves from the 1960s' *Batman* television series. The "exotic" location has appeared in countless films, as well—from sci-fi B-movies *(Teenagers from Outer Space),* to westerns *(The Searchers),* to historical epics *(Julius Caesar). Canyon Dr. & Brush Canyon Trail. Take the Canyon Dr. entrance, and then hike .25 miles past the parking lot.*

2 ★★★ kids Observatory. After trying out a powerful telescope at nearby Mount Wilson, Griffith experienced an epiphany: "If all mankind could look through that telescope, it would change the world!" With that noble goal, he left the city money to create the Griffith Observatory, which debuted in 1935. The original 12-inch Zeiss refracting telescope, which more people have looked through than any other on earth, remains in prime condition and serves up to 600 visitors nightly. In the other copper-topped dome is the triple-beam solar telescope, which is used to observe the sun safely. The recent renovation added 40,000 square feet of slick, but accessible, exhibits like "The Edge of Space," which displays Martian and lunar meteorites. A timed-entry reservation is required to enter the Observatory. ⏱ *1–2 hr. 2800 E. Observatory Rd.* ☎ *213/473-0800. www.griffithobservatory.org. Tues–Fri noon–10pm, Sat–Sun 10am–10pm. Go to 5333 Zoo Dr. for Observatory reservations & shuttle rides.*

3 ★ Planetarium. The freshly overhauled Samuel Oschin Planetarium offers a state-of-the-art, star-studded experience called "Centered in the Universe," which lets the viewer experience the Big Bang,

A monument to James Dean, who helped make the Griffith Observatory world famous in Rebel Without a Cause.

travel distant galaxies, and observe the overall structure of the universe—all without leaving his or her cushy seat. *Note:* Entry to the planetarium is not included with the shuttle or entry tickets. Tickets can only be purchased at the Observatory, and they often sell out; try to buy tickets immediately upon your arrival. *www. griffithobservatory.org. Tues–Fri noon–10pm, Sat–Sun 10am–10pm. $7 adults & children over 13, $5 seniors, $3 children 5–12. Children under 5 are not admitted. Check website for planetarium showtimes.*

4 kids **Travel Town Museum.** In the late 1940s, park employee Charley Atkins and a few of his train-loving pals decided to create a "railroad petting zoo" to encourage kids to become engineers. Young kids, especially Thomas the Tank Engine fans, love exploring the steam-powered engines, vintage railcars, and cabooses. A miniature-train ride costs $2.50. For more train fun, head over to the Griffith Park & Southern Railroad (4400 Crystal Springs Dr.) on the other side of the park. *5200 Zoo Dr.* ☎ *323/662-9678. www.traveltown.org. Mon–Fri 10am–4pm, Sat–Sun 10am–5pm. Free admission.*

5 kids ★ **Los Angeles Zoo and Botanical Gardens.** The zoo continues to improve its exhibits: In 2009 a new "Pachyderm

Visiting with kids? Be sure to stop at the Los Angeles Zoo.

Ornate revolvers on display at Gene Autry's Museum of the American West.

Forest" will expand the elephant space into one of the largest in the country; in 2010 "Rainforest of the Americas" will present mixed species (mammals, reptiles, birds, and insects) in a tropical setting intended to immerse the visitor in a sensory experience, with a central theme of water, the rainforest's key ingredient. *5333 Zoo Dr., Griffith Park.* ☎ *323/644-4200. www.lazoo.org. $10 adults, $7 seniors, $5 children 2–12, free for kids under 2. Daily 10am–5pm (July 1–Labor Day till 6pm).*

6 kids **Gene Autry's Museum of the American West.** This is no podunk outpost, but a well-kept museum that explores the "real" Old West as well as the mythology perpetuated by movies and television. Past exhibits have included George Catlin's "Indian Gallery," hundreds of paintings from the 1830s by the first artist to document the Plains Indians in their own territories; "Dazzling Firearms," decorative pistols from the 19th and 20th centuries; and "Once Upon a Time in Italy," a celebration of the spaghetti westerns by Sergio Leone. *4700 Western Heritage Way.* ☎ *323/667-2000. Tues–Sun 10am–5pm, Thurs 10am–8pm. $9 adults, $5 students & seniors, $3 children 3–12, free for children under 3.*

End your day with a sunset horseback ride at Sunset Ranch.

7 kids **Merry-Go-Round.** Safe (for now) from recent wildfires, the carousel has delighted families since 1937. Jumping horses, bejeweled and brightly colored, spin around to the sounds of marches and waltzes from a Stinson band organ. ☎ *323/665-3051. Weekends & summer weekdays 11am–5pm. $1.50 rides. Head to Park Center, located between the zoo & the Los Feliz entrance.*

8 **Golf.** Got time to hit the links? The park is home to two popular 18-hole public golf courses, Wilson and Harding, as well as a driving range and practice putting greens. There's also the 9-hole Roosevelt course at 2650 N. Vermont Ave. *4730 Crystal Springs Dr. ☎ 323/663-2555. Sunrise–11pm. Head east on Los Feliz Blvd. & north at the Riverside entrance.*

9 **Greek Theatre.** Another gift from Griffith J. Griffith, this 5,700-seat venue debuted in 1930. Tree-lined and nestled in the hills, the award-winning theater feels like an intimate version of the Hollywood Bowl. Recent acts have included Tony Bennett, Beastie Boys, Stevie Wonder, Air, and Radiohead. *2700 Vermont Canyon Rd. ☎ 323/665-1927. www.greektheatrela.com.*

10 **Sunset Ranch Dinner Ride.** Mount up and mosey through the twilight over the hills to a Mexican restaurant in Burbank. Take it easy on the margaritas, cowboy—you still have to ride the horse back. *3400 Beachwood Dr. ☎ 323/469-5450. www.sunsetranchhollywood. com. Dinner ride on Fri only. Sign up at 4:30pm (first come, first served); hit the trails at 5:30pm. $60 adults (does not include dinner or drinks). Head north up Beachwood Dr.*

Huntington Library & Gardens

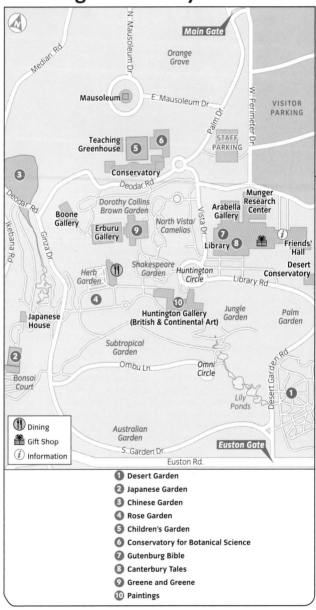

Main Gate

Orange Grove

Median Rd.

N. Mausoleum Dr.

Mausoleum

E. Mausoleum Dr.

VISITOR PARKING

W. Perimeter Dr.

Palm Dr.

STAFF PARKING

Teaching Greenhouse **5** **6**

Conservatory

Deodar Rd.

3

Deodar Rd.

Ikebana Rd.

Ginza Dr.

Dorothy Collins Brown Garden

Boone Gallery

Erburu Gallery **9**

North Vista/ Camelias

Vista Dr.

Munger Research Center

Arabella Gallery

7 **8**
Library 🎁 *(i)* Friends' Hall

Desert Conservatory

Herb Garden 🍴

Shakespeare Garden

4

Huntington Circle

10

Library Rd.

Japanese House

Huntington Gallery (British & Continental Art)

Jungle Garden

Palm Garden

2

Bonsai Court

Subtropical Garden

Ombu Ln.

Omni Circle

Desert Garden Rd.

1

Lily Ponds

🍴 Dining
🎁 Gift Shop
(i) Information

Australian Garden

S. Garden Dr.

Euston Gate

Euston Rd.

1 Desert Garden
2 Japanese Garden
3 Chinese Garden
4 Rose Garden
5 Children's Garden
6 Conservatory for Botanical Science
7 Gutenburg Bible
8 Canterbury Tales
9 Greene and Greene
10 Paintings

Upon his death in 1927, railroad and real-estate tycoon Henry E. Huntington willed that his private 207-acre estate, near Pasadena, be opened to the public as a library, museum, and botanical gardens—now a triple-shot of world-class attractions. With 15,000 species of plants landscaped across 120 acres, the magnificent gardens are best enjoyed at a leisurely pace (closing time is 4:30pm, and you'll need 2 hr. at the very least). *Tip:* The Rose Garden Tea Room is quaint, but for high tea the way it was meant to be, I recommend the sumptuous Ritz-Carlton Huntington (p 147) a few blocks away. *1151 Oxford Rd., San Marino.* ☎ *626/405-2100. www.huntington.org. Tues–Fri noon–4:30pm, Sat–Sun 10:30am– 4:30pm. $15 adults, $12 seniors 65 & up, $10 students & children 12 & up, $6 children 5–11, free for children under 5. Free for everyone the 1st Thurs of the month.*

① ★ **Desert Garden.** Two dozen families of succulents, many imported from the Southwest and Mexican deserts, occupy 10 acres, making it one of the largest collections of its kind in the world. *Warning:* The gorgeous display can be a black hole for photography enthusiasts, who insist on "just one more" extreme close-up of a blooming ocotillo.

② ★★★ **Japanese Garden.** True to Japanese tradition, this garden is a harmonious and multi-faceted retreat, created through the disciplined interplay between the elements of water, rocks, and plants. Highlights include a stroll garden, picturesque moon bridge, Shoin-style house, and Bonsai court.

③ **Chinese Garden.** Set to open in mid-2008, the 12-acre site takes its construction cues from ancient China: Eight pavilions, including a tea house, will surround a 1-acre lake, and will be linked by winding pathways designed to draw the visitor through a series of "poetic views." Key architectural elements— sculpted rocks, handcrafted lattice windows, and roof tiles—are being imported from China.

Succulents in the Desert Garden.

The Best of the Outdoors

Make time for a pass through the impressive Rose Garden.

④ ★ **Rose Garden.** If you're like me and thought that roses only came in two varieties, red or not red, you're in for a shock: Here are 1,200 cultivars in a kaleidoscope of colors. To catch them in full bloom—between late April and early June—is breathtaking.

⑤ **Children's Garden.** The area is specifically designed to tickle the curiosity of children ages 2 to 7. Kinetic sculptures, water bells, a tunnel of prisms, misty rainbows, magnetic sand, a fog grotto—each of the hands-on experiences explores one or more of the four ancient elements: fire, water, earth, and air.

⑥ **Conservatory for Botanical Science.** Older children and adults enjoy the 16,000-square-foot, award-winning conservatory. It features interactive botanical exhibits, none more popular than the Amorphophallis titanium, better known as the "Stinky Flower."

⑦ ★★★ **Gutenberg Bible.** With more than six million rare books and manuscripts, the Huntington is one of the largest research libraries in the world. Perhaps the most famous item on public display is a 1455 Gutenberg Bible, one of only 12 vellum (fine parchment, as opposed to paper) copies in the world. *Library Exhibition Hall.*

⑧ ★ **Canterbury Tales.** Created around 1410, the Ellesmere manuscript of Chaucer's *Canterbury Tales* features 464 pages of cursive text with floral borders and other meticulous decorations, such as 23 portraits of the pilgrim-storytellers, including Chaucer himself. Scholars consider it to be one of the most significant English-language manuscripts in existence.

⑨ **Greene and Greene.** An excellent companion to a tour of the Greenes' Gamble House in Pasadena (their Arts and Crafts masterpiece; p 37), this permanent installation displays Greene-designed tables, chairs, lamps, and rugs. *Virginia Steele Scott Gallery of American Art.*

⑩ **Paintings.** Henry's wife Arabella was the driving force behind the comprehensive collection of British and French art of the 18th and 19th centuries. Two highlights are the portraits that seem to be checking each other out: Thomas Gainsborough's *The Blue Boy* and Thomas Lawrence's *Pinkie.* *Huntington Gallery.* ●

Chaucer's Canterbury Tales *is one of the highlights of Huntington Library & Gardens.*

Dining Best Bets

Best Italian
★★★ Angelini Osteria $$$ 7313 Beverly Blvd. (p 105)

Best of the Best
★★★ AOC $$$ 8022 W. Third St. (p 105)

Best Burger
★★★ Apple Pan $ 10801 W. Pico Blvd. (p 105); and ★★ Father's Office $$ 1018 Montana Ave. (p 107)

Best Brunch
★★★ Campanile $$ 624 S. La Brea Ave. (p 105)

Best Movie Set Interior
★★★ Cicada $$$ 617 S. Olive St. (p 106)

Best Steak
★★ Dan Tana's $$$ 9071 Santa Monica Blvd. (p 106); and ★★★ Mastro's $$$$ 246 N. Canon Dr. (p 109)

Best Dim Sum
★★ Empress Pavilion $ 988 N. Hill St. (p 107)

Best Date Night
★★ Grace $$$ 7360 Beverly Blvd. (p 107); and ★★ Hatfield's $$$ 7458 Beverly Blvd. (p 107)

Best Fine Dining
★★★ Josie $$$ 2424 Pico Blvd. (p 108)

Best Sushi
★★★ Katsu-Ya $$ 11680 Ventura Blvd. (p 108)

Best Lunch at the Farmer's Market
★★ Loteria! Grill $ 6333 W. Third St. (p 108)

Best Seafood
★★★ Malibu Seafood $ 25653 Pacific Coast Hwy. (p 108); and ★★★ Water Grill $$$ 544 S. Grand Ave. (p 112)

Best Pre-Theater Meal
★★★ Patina $$$$ 141 S. Grand Ave. (p 110)

Best Vietnamese
★ Pho Café $ 2841 W. Sunset Blvd. (p 110)

Most Worth the Wait
★★★ Pizzeria Mozza $$$ 641 N. Highland Ave. (p 110)

Best Tacos
★ Yuca's $ 2056 Hillhurst Ave. (p 112)

The French-dipped sandwich and the sawdust floor are the trademarks of Philippe The Original.

Santa Monica & the Beaches

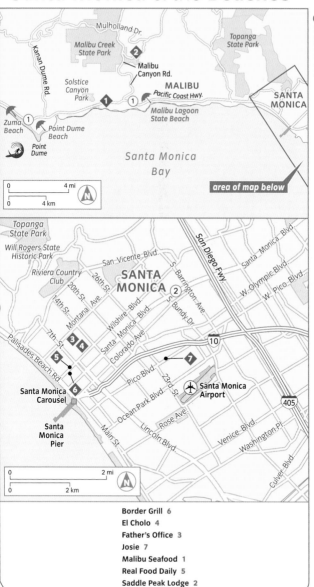

Border Grill 6
El Cholo 4
Father's Office 3
Josie 7
Malibu Seafood 1
Real Food Daily 5
Saddle Peak Lodge 2

P 99: At the Border Grill in Santa Monica.

Beverly Hills & the Westside

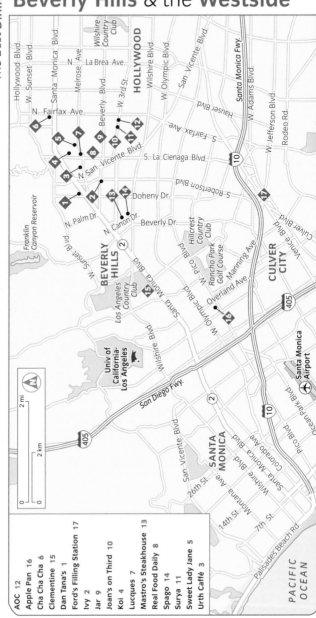

AOC 12
Apple Pan 16
Cha Cha Cha 6
Clementine 15
Dan Tana's 1
Ford's Filling Station 17
Ivy 2
Jar 9
Joan's on Third 10
Koi 4
Lucques 7
Mastro's Steakhouse 13
Real Food Daily 8
Spago 14
Surya 11
Sweet Lady Jane 5
Urth Caffé 3

Hollywood, Los Feliz & Silver Lake

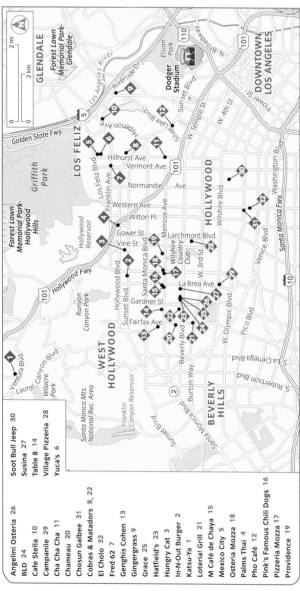

Downtown

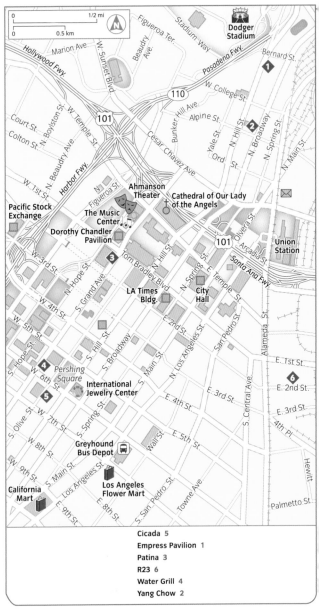

Cicada 5
Empress Pavilion 1
Patina 3
R23 6
Water Grill 4
Yang Chow 2

Dining A to Z

★★★ Angelini Osteria WEST HOLLYWOOD *ITALIAN* Chef/owner Gino Angelini brings Roma right to your plate with fresh ingredients and his *mamma*'s authentic recipes. The small, unpretentious room gets loud, but that's what amazing food does to people. Another good sign: The crowd often includes Italians and off-duty chefs. *7313 Beverly Blvd., at Poinsettia Place.* ☎ *323/297-0070. Reservations recommended. Entrees $12–$38. AE, MC, V. Lunch & dinner Tues–Sun. Map p 103.*

★★★ AOC WEST HOLLYWOOD *CALIFORNIA/FRENCH* Foodies huddle over small plates—charcuterie, cheese (French, Italian, and Spanish), skirt steak, fried oysters—and sip on sublime wines in a casual, chic setting. *8022 W. Third St., at Crescent Heights Blvd.* ☎ *323/653-6359. Reservations recommended. Small plates $9–$18. AE, MC, V. Dinner daily. Map p 102.*

★★★ Apple Pan WESTWOOD *BURGERS* Built in 1947, this old-school burger joint still knows how to serve 'em up. Chase your hickory burger with a slab of apple pie. *10801 W. Pico Blvd., at Glendon Ave.* ☎ *310/ 475-3585. Burgers $7. Cash only. Lunch & dinner Tues–Sun. Map p 102.*

★★ kids BLD WEST HOLLYWOOD *NEW AMERICAN* A popular new cafe from Grace's Neal Fraser, BLD pushes typical diner fare into something far tastier for breakfast, lunch, and dinner (get it?). *7450 Beverly Blvd., at N. Vista St.* ☎ *323/930-9744. Entrees $4–$26. AE, MC, V. Breakfast, lunch & dinner daily. Map p 103.*

★ kids Border Grill SANTA MONICA *LATIN* The Food Network's *Too Hot Tamales*, Mary Sue Milliken and Susan Feniger, present gourmet Mexican cuisine in a fiesta-like atmosphere (read: it can get *loud*). Tres leches cake is a must for dessert. *1445 Fourth St., at Santa Monica Blvd.* ☎ *310/451-1655. Entrees $13–$25. AE, MC, V. Lunch & dinner daily. Map p 101.*

Cafe Stella SILVER LAKE *FRENCH* The food here isn't quite *ooh la la,* but it's good enough to sustain the charming and romantic vibe of a Parisian cafe. Great wine and a sometimes brusque staff seal its Frenchness. *3932 Sunset Blvd., at Hyperion Ave.* ☎ *323/666-0265. Entrees $12–$20. AE, MC, V. Dinner daily. Map p 103.*

★★★ kids Campanile HOLLYWOOD *CALIFORNIA/MEDITERRANEAN* In a 1928 Tuscan-style building that once belonged to Charlie Chaplin, Mark Peel's restaurant has made history on its own for nearly 20 years as one of the city's best restaurants. Grilled Cheese Night is a popular draw on Thursdays, but nothing beats the delicious weekend brunch in the sunny courtyard. *624 S. La Brea Ave., at Wilshire Blvd.* ☎ *323/938-1447. Reservations recommended. Entrees $10–$38. AE, MC, V. Lunch & dinner Mon–Sat, brunch Sun. Map p 103.*

★ kids Cha Cha Cha SILVER LAKE *CARIBBEAN* If you like your brunches fun and festive, go for the

A shrimp dish at AOC.

The festive interior of Cha Cha Cha.

jerk chicken omelet, churros, and sangria at this colorful spot. *656 N. Virgil Ave., at Clinton St.* ☎ *323/664-7723. Also in West Hollywood at 7953 Santa Monica Blvd., at Fairfax Ave.* ☎ *323/848-7700. Entrees $8–$13. AE, MC, V. Breakfast, lunch & dinner daily. Maps p 102 and p 103.*

★★ **Chameau** FAIRFAX *MOROCCAN* Step inside the whimsical mod-meets-Moroccan interior, and you know you're in for something different. The cuisine is French-Moroccan, emphasizing robust flavors and seasonal ingredients. The *bastilla* and the *tagine* are across-the-board favorites. *339 N. Fairfax Ave., at Beverly Blvd. & Oakwood Ave.* ☎ *323/951-0039. Entrees $12–$20. AE, MC, V. Dinner Tues–Sat. Map p 103.*

★ **Chosun Galbee** KOREATOWN *KOREAN BBQ* The fresh, savory meats will delight any Korean BBQ connoisseur, while the spotless, sleek interior (polished steel, smoked glass, and slate floors) will ease new-bies who are unfamiliar with tabletop cooking. *3330 W. Olympic Blvd., at Western Ave.* ☎ *323/734-3330. Entrees $12–$30. AE, MC, V. Lunch Mon–Fri, dinner daily. Map p 103.*

★★★ **Cicada** DOWNTOWN *NORTH-ERN ITALIAN* Enjoy fine Italian dining in one of the city's most stunning Art Deco environments with Lalique glass doors, rich wood columns and paneling, a gold-leaf ceiling, and a grand stairway. No wonder most weekends are booked for weddings. *617 S. Olive St., btwn Sixth & Seventh sts.* ☎ *213/488-9488. Reservations recommended. Entrees $20–$40. AE, MC, V. Dinner Mon–Thurs. Map p 104.*

★★ **Clementine** CENTURY CITY *BAKERY/SANDWICHES* This casual cafe and bakery wins you over by doing all the simple things right. Scones, salads, sandwiches, and soups are all delish. Only downside: parking. *1751 Ensley Ave., at Santa Monica Blvd.* ☎ *310/552-1080. Entrees $8–$12. AE, MC, V. Breakfast, lunch & dinner Mon–Fri, dinner Sat. Map p 102.*

★★ **Cobras & Matadors** WEST HOLLYWOOD *SPANISH TAPAS* This cozy charmer is great for small plates and hot dates. Once you finally sit down and order, the food can fly out fast: gazpacho, sweet potato fries, albondigas, Spanish cheeses, barbecued skirt steak, Serrano ham and Manchego croquettes, and churros with a chocolate dipping sauce. *7615 W. Beverly Blvd., btwn Fairfax & La Brea aves.* ☎ *323/932-6178. Also in Los Feliz at 4655 Hollywood Blvd., at Vermont Ave.* ☎ *323/669-3922. Reservations recommended. Small plates $7–$15. AE, MC, V. Dinner daily. Map p 103.*

★★ **Dan Tana's** WEST HOLLYWOOD *ITALIAN* This dark and cozy hole-in-the-wall, a West Hollywood fixture since 1964, cooks up classic steaks and hearty Italian dishes for a multi-generational mix of industry heavyweights, actors, rockers, hangers-on, and wannabes. *9071 Santa Monica Blvd., at Doheny Dr.* ☎ *310/275-9444. Reservations recommended. Entrees*

$20–$56. AE, MC, V. Dinner daily. Map p 102.

★ **El Cholo** KOREATOWN MEXICAN Try the green corn tamales at L.A.'s oldest Mexican restaurant, which has drawn its share of celebs since 1927. 1121 S. Western Ave. (btwn 11th & 12th sts.). ☎ 323/734-2773. Also in Santa Monica at 1025 Wilshire Blvd., at 11th St. ☎ 310/899-1106. Entrees $10–$14. AE, MC, V. Lunch & dinner daily. Maps p 101 and 103.

★★ **Empress Pavilion** CHINA-TOWN DIM SUM For dim sum this good, you'll end up waiting for a table even though the massive dining room seats 600 people. 988 N. Hill St., at Bernard St. ☎ 213/617-9898. Entrees $8–$12. AE, MC, V. Dinner daily. Map p 104.

★★ **Father's Office** SANTA MON-ICA CONTEMPORARY CALIFORNIAN This pub is packed with folks clamoring for the famous burger, served one way—Gruyère and Maytag blue cheese, caramelized onions, smoked bacon compote, on a French roll. 1018 Montana Ave., at 10th St. ☎ 310/393-2337. Reservations not accepted; minors not admitted. Entrees $5–$15. Lunch Sat, dinner daily. AE, M, V. Map p 101.

★ **Ford's Filling Station** CULVER CITY NEW AMERICAN Since opening in 2006, Ben Ford's gastropub has been a solid hit, with dishes like fried Ipswich clams, organic sirloin burgers, fish and chips, and crispy flattened chicken. 9531 Culver Blvd., at Irving Place. ☎ 310/202-1470. Entrees $12–$25. AE, MC, V. Lunch Mon–Fri, dinner Mon–Sat. Map p 102.

★ kids **Fred 62** LOS FELIZ DINER A favorite among eastside hipsters, this retro-styled diner always hits its mark—Bearded Mr. Frenchy (cornflake-encrusted French toast), Thai Cobb salad, or a mean tuna melt for late-night munchies. 1850 N. Vermont Ave., at Russell Ave. ☎ 323/667-0062. Entrees $8–$12. AE, MC, V. Breakfast, lunch & dinner daily 24 hr. Map p 103.

★ **Genghis Cohen** WEST HOLLY-WOOD CHINESE Nothing too trendy here, just good New York–style Chinese food served in a comfortable, refreshingly unhip setting. 740 N. Fairfax Ave., at Melrose Ave. ☎ 323/653-0640. Entrees $11–$26. AE, MC, V. Lunch & dinner daily. Map p 103.

★ kids **Gingergrass** SILVER LAKE VIETNAMESE Try the Bo Sate and the spring rolls at this hip and bustling Silver Lake favorite. 2396 Glendale Blvd. ☎ 323/644-1600. Entrees $10–$15. AE, MC, V. Lunch & dinner daily. Map p 103.

★★ **Grace** WEST HOLLYWOOD NEW AMERICAN Neal Fraser's lovely restaurant has earned a reputation as one of the best dining experiences in town, with fine cuisine in a warm atmosphere. Try Doughnut Shoppe Wednesdays. 7360 Beverly Blvd., at Fuller Ave. ☎ 323/934-4400. Reservations recommended. Entrees $15–$40. AE, MC, V. Dinner Tues–Sun. Map p 103.

★★ **Hatfield's** WEST HOLLYWOOD NEW AMERICAN Spare but charming, this place is all about the sophisticated, seasonal menu from husband-and-wife chef team, Quinn and Karen Hatfield. Raves go to the charred Japanese octopus and

At Cobras & Matadors, the specialty is tapas (small plates).

the sugar-and-spice beignets. *7458 Beverly Blvd., at Gardner St.* ☎ *323/ 935-2977. Reservations recommended. Entrees $29–$38. AE, MC, V. Dinner Mon–Sat. Map p 103.*

★★ Hungry Cat HOLLYWOOD
SEAFOOD If you forgive the odd location in the shadow of a retail behemoth, you can enjoy fantastic cocktails and inventive, well-executed seafood. *1535 N. Vine St., at Sunset Blvd.* ☎ *323/462-2155. Entrees $13–$45. AE, MC, V. Lunch Sun–Fri, dinner daily. Map p 103.*

★★★ kids In-N-Out Burger HOL-
LYWOOD *BURGERS* With the freshest ingredients and no microwaves or freezers, this is the best fast-food burger in California. *7009 Sunset Blvd., at Orange Dr.* ☎ *800/786-1000. Multiple other locations. Burgers $4. AE, MC, V. Lunch & dinner daily. Map p 103.*

★ Ivy BEVERLY HILLS NEW AMERI-
CAN With the paparazzi camped outside the white picket-fenced patio, this spot serves upscale comfort food to stars, power brokers, and tourists. *113 N. Robertson Blvd. (btwn Beverly Blvd. & Third St.).* ☎ *310/274-8303. Reservations recommended. Entrees $10–$38. AE, MC, V. Lunch & dinner daily. Map p 102.*

★★ Jar WEST HOLLYWOOD NEW
AMERICAN Stylish and elegant, this steakhouse boasts superb service and a knockout Sunday brunch including chilaquiles with crème fraîche, and pecan sweet bread. *8225 Beverly Blvd., at Harper Ave.* ☎ *323/ 655-6566. Entrees $11–$27. AE, MC, V. Dinner daily, brunch Sun. Map p 102.*

★★ Joan's on Third WEST HOLLY-
WOOD *BAKERY/SANDWICHES* This bakery and deluxe deli stocks a variety of gourmet salads and sandwiches, and to-die-for cupcakes. A perfect pit stop when shopping on Third Street. *8350 W. Third St., at Kings Rd.* ☎ *323/655-2285. Sandwiches & salads $10–$13. AE, MC, V. Lunch & dinner daily. Map p 102.*

★★★ Josie SANTA MONICA NEW
AMERICAN Gourmands seek out Josie Le Balch's nuanced American cuisine with French and Italian flair. *2424 Pico Blvd., at 25th St.* ☎ *310/ 581-9888. Reservations recommended. Entrees $25–$38. AE, MC, V. Dinner daily. Map p 101.*

★★★ Katsu-Ya STUDIO CITY
SUSHI Don't be a valley snob— you have to try the spicy tuna on crispy rice and the amazing baked crab rolls. *11680 Ventura Blvd., at Colfax Ave.* ☎ *818/985-6976. Reservations recommended. Sushi & rolls $4–$12. AE, MC, V. Sushi & rolls daily. Map p 103.*

★ Koi WEST HOLLYWOOD SUSHI
The sushi is good, but people come for the "scene"—the young and the beautiful trying to be in the right place at the right time. *730 N. La Cienega Blvd. (btwn Melrose & Willoughby aves.).* ☎ *310/659-9449. Reservations recommended. Entrees $13–$27. AE, MC, V. Dinner daily. Map p 102.*

Cupcakes at Joan's on Third.

The chic dining room of Koi.

★★ kids Loteria! Grill FARMERS MARKET *MEXICAN* This unassuming Mexican stand draws lines of locals with fast, friendly service and authentic food. *6333 W. Third St., at Fairfax Ave.* ☎ *323/930-2211. Entrees $7–$12. MC, V. Breakfast, lunch & dinner daily. Map p 103.*

★★ Lucques WEST HOLLYWOOD *CALIFORNIA* This revered restaurant offers a small but sophisticated menu of French-Mediterranean dishes. Request a patio table. *8474 Melrose Ave., at La Cienega Blvd.* ☎ *323/655-6277. Reservations recommended. Entrees $16–$44. AE, MC, V. Lunch Tues–Sat, dinner daily. Map p 102.*

★ M Café de Chaya WEST HOLLYWOOD *VEGETARIAN* If "flavorful macrobiotic" sounds oxymoronic to you, prepare to be surprisingly satisfied by the panini and rice bowls at this hot spot for starlets and the health-obsessed. *7119 Melrose Ave., at La Brea Ave.* ☎ *323/525-0588. Entrees $5–$14. AE, MC, V. Breakfast, lunch & dinner daily. Map p 103.*

★★★ kids Malibu Seafood MALIBU *SEAFOOD* Just a stone's throw from the Pacific, this walk-up-and-order shack serves some of the freshest seafood on the coast. You

can't miss with fish and chips or lobster. *25653 Pacific Coast Hwy. (1½ miles north of Malibu Canyon Rd.).* ☎ *310/456-3430. Entrees $5–$20. MC, V. Lunch & dinner daily. Map p 101.*

★★★ Mastro's Steakhouse BEVERLY HILLS *STEAK* Score a martini and a perfectly grilled double porterhouse at this swank, low-lit steakhouse in the heart of Beverly Hills. Somewhere, the Rat Pack is smiling. *246 N. Canon Dr. (btwn Clifton & Dayton ways).* ☎ *310/888-8782. Reservations recommended. Entrees $26–$63. AE, MC, V. Dinner daily. Map p 102.*

A plate is prepared at Lucques.

★★ **kids** **Mexico City** LOS FELIZ *MEXICAN* Friendly and fun, this is my absolute favorite place in L.A. for margaritas and enchiladas. *2121 Hillhurst Ave., at Avocado St.* ☎ *323/661-7227. Entrees $8–$15. AE, MC, V. Lunch Wed–Sun, dinner daily. Map p 103.*

★★★ **Osteria Mozza** HOLLY-WOOD *ITALIAN* After opening the casual Pizzeria Mozza next door, the formidable team of Nancy Silverton and Mario Batali went upscale with this sleek Italian restaurant, currently the hottest ticket in town. *6602 Melrose Ave., at Highland Ave.* ☎ *323/297-0100. Reservations recommended. Entrees $15–$45. AE, MC, V. Dinner Mon–Sat. Map p 103.*

★ **Palms Thai** THAI TOWN *THAI* Gobble up authentic Thai specialties while the Thai Elvis croons the classics. *5900 Hollywood Blvd., at Bronson St.* ☎ *323/462-5073. Entrees $5–$20. AE, MC, V. Lunch & dinner daily. Map p 103.*

★★★ **Patina** DOWNTOWN *NEW AMERICAN* For a world-class dining experience, book a table in this stunning space in the Walt Disney Concert Hall. *141 S. Grand Ave., at Second St. (in Walt Disney Concert Hall).* ☎ *213/972-3331. www.patinagroup.com*

At Pho Café, in Silver Lake.

Reservations recommended. Entrees $36–$44. AE, MC, V. Lunch Tues–Fri, dinner daily. Map p 104.

★ **Pho Café** SILVER LAKE *VIET-NAMESE* The Vietnamese noodle soups and crepes are fresh, cheap, and unbelievably tasty. The lack of a sign lets you know it's too cool for its random strip-mall location. *2841 W. Sunset Blvd., at Silver Lake Blvd.* ☎ *213/413-0888. Entrees $5–$10. Cash only. Lunch & dinner daily. Map p 103.*

★ **Pink's Famous Chili Dogs** HOLLYWOOD *HOT DOGS* Slinging hot dogs since 1939, Pink's occupies a special place in Hollywood's cholesterol-laden heart. *709 N. La Brea Ave., at Melrose Ave.* ☎ *323/931-4223. Dogs & burgers $3–$7. Cash only. Breakfast, lunch & dinner daily. Map p 103.*

★★★ **Pizzeria Mozza** HOLLY-WOOD *PIZZA* This highbrow pizzeria has foodies fighting for tables. The pizza's distinctive crust, puffy and crispy, sets the stage for artisanal toppings—squash blossoms, littleneck clams, or, my favorite, fennel sausage. *641 N. Highland Ave., at Melrose Ave.* ☎ *323/297-0101. Reservations recommended. Entrees $10–$25. AE, MC, V. Lunch & dinner daily. Map p 103.*

★★★ **Providence** HOLLYWOOD *SEAFOOD* Known for its exquisitely prepared seafood, this restaurant is considered to be one of the best in the country. *5955 Melrose Ave., at Cole Ave.* ☎ *323/460-4170. Entrees $25–$48. AE, MC, V. Lunch Fri, dinner daily. Map p 103.*

★ **R23** DOWNTOWN *SUSHI* This arty spot with cardboard chairs is the best sushi Downtown, albeit slightly hard to find. *E. Second St. (btwn Alameda St. & Santa Fe Ave.).* ☎ *213/687-7178. Entrees $15–$30. Lunch Mon–Fri, dinner Mon–Sat. Map p 104.*

Pink's is popular with the late-night crowd.

★ **kids Real Food Daily** WEST HOLLYWOOD *VEGETARIAN* How do some celebs stay so slim? This delicious vegan cuisine might be one reason. *414 N. La Cienega Blvd. (btwn Beverly Blvd. & Melrose Ave.). ☎ 310/289-9910. Also in Santa Monica at 514 Santa Monica Blvd., at Fifth St. ☎ 310/451-7544. Entrees $7–$15. AE, MC, V. Lunch & dinner daily. Map p 101.*

★★ **Saddle Peak Lodge** CAL-ABASAS *NEW AMERICAN/GAME* This former hunting lodge is worth the drive to the Malibu hills for its rustic beauty and fabulous game. *419 Cold Canyon Rd., at Piuma Rd. ☎ 818/222-3888. Reservations recommended. Entrees $28–$42. AE, MC, V. Dinner Wed–Sun, brunch Sat–Sun. Map p 101.*

★★ **Soot Bull Jeep** KOREATOWN *KOREAN BBQ* Indifferent service, smoky air, and down-and-dirty decor—none of this matters; the charcoal grill at your table gives the meat its smoky, delectable flavor. *3136 Eighth St., at Catalina St.*

☎ 213/387-3865. Entrees $12–$25. AE, MC, V. Lunch & dinner daily. Map p 103.

★ **Spago** BEVERLY HILLS *CALIFOR-NIA* Wolfgang Puck's groundbreaking restaurant continues to live up to its hype. Make it easy on yourself and order the tasting menu. *176 N. Canon Dr., at Wilshire Blvd. ☎ 310/385-0880. Reservations recommended. Entrees $17–$66, tasting menu $125. AE, MC, V. Lunch & dinner daily. Map p 102.*

★★ **Surya** WEST HOLLYWOOD *INDIAN* Routinely rated among the best Indian restaurants in town, Surya is also one of the friendliest. *8048 W. Third St., at Crescent Heights Blvd. ☎ 323/653-5151. Entrees $10–$22. AE, MC, V. Dinner daily. Map p 102.*

★★ **kids Susina** WEST HOLLY-WOOD *BAKERY* With a gorgeous array of pastries and desserts, the toughest part will be making up your mind. Great quiche and panini, too. *7122 Beverly Blvd., at La Brea Ave. ☎ 323/934-7900. Pastries & entrees $2–$7. AE, MC, V. Breakfast, lunch & dinner daily. Map p 103.*

★★★ **Sweet Lady Jane** WEST HOLLYWOOD *BAKERY/DESSERT* These scrumptious cakes and cupcakes are big hits for parties and

Game, such as the ostrich meat pictured here, is the draw at Saddle Peak Lodge.

gifts. Try the Tripleberry. *8360 Melrose Ave., at N. Kings Rd.* ☎ *323/653-7145. Sandwiches & desserts $6.50–$10. Mon–Sat. Map p 102.*

★★★ **Table 8** WEST HOLLYWOOD *CALIFORNIA* Chef Govind Armstrong presents innovative California cuisine in a dark and cozy environment. *7661 Melrose Ave., at Spaulding Ave.* ☎ *323/782-8258. Reservations recommended. Entrees $26–$38. AE, MC, V. Dinner Mon–Sat. Map p 103.*

★ **Urth Caffé** WEST HOLLYWOOD *BAKERY/SANDWICHES* Enjoy the sunny patio of this health-conscious cafe, which takes pride (justifiably) in its organic coffee and teas. Bedraggled Hollywood types trying to counteract the excesses of the previous night are lured by the all-natural ingredients in the gourmet salads, quiches, panini, and guilt-free pastries. *8565 Melrose Ave., at Westmount Dr.* ☎ *310/659-0628. Entrees $5.95–$13. AE, MC, V. Breakfast, lunch & dinner daily. Map p 102.*

★ **kids Village Pizzeria** LARCHMONT *PIZZA* This small, family-owned shop brings New York–style pizza to the Larchmont Village. *131 N. Larchmont Blvd. (btwn Beverly Blvd. & First St.).* ☎ *323/465-5566. Pizzas $11–$20. AE, MC, V. Lunch & dinner daily. Map p 103.*

★★★ **Water Grill** DOWNTOWN *SEAFOOD* Seafood lovers and Downtown concert-goers flock to this revered restaurant known for its shellfish. *544 S. Grand Ave. (btwn Fifth & Sixth sts.).* ☎ *213/891-0900. www.watergrill.com. Entrees $12–$40. Reservations recommended. AE, MC, V. Lunch Mon–Fri, dinner Mon–Sat. Map p 104.*

★★ **Yang Chow** CHINATOWN *CHINESE* Try the signature slippery shrimp at this top-rated Mandarin and Szechuan spot in Chinatown. *819 N. Broadway, at Alpine St.* ☎ *213/625-0811. Reservations recommended. Entrees $10–$15. AE, MC, V. Lunch & dinner daily. Map p 104.*

★ **Yuca's** LOS FELIZ *TACOS* This street-side, family-owned hut is a taco-lover's paradise. Most popular are the carnitas and the carne asada. *2056 Hillhurst Ave., at Ambrose Ave.* ☎ *323/662-1214. Tacos & burritos $3–$6. Cash only. Lunch Mon–Sat. Map p 103.* ●

Stop by Urth Caffé for a healthful snack or meal.

Nightlife Best Bets

Best Burlesque
★★★ 40 Deuce, *5574 Melrose Ave.*
(p 122)

Best Jukebox
★★ 4100 Bar, *4100 Sunset Blvd.*
(p 118)

Best Manicure with a Cosmo
★ Beauty Bar, *1638 N. Cahuenga*
Blvd. (p 118)

Best Happy Hour
★ The Cat and Fiddle, *6530 W.*
Sunset Blvd. (p 118)

Best Dive Bar
★ Frolic Room, *6245 Hollywood*
Blvd. (p 120)

Best Lounge Act
★ Marty and Elaine at The Dresden, *1760 N. Vermont Ave. (p 118)*

Best Gay & Lesbian
★ East/West Lounge, *801 Larrabee*
St. (p 121)

Most Historic Bar
★★★ Formosa Cafe, *7156 Santa*
Monica Blvd. (p 118)

Best Downtown Bar
★ Golden Gopher, *417 W. Eighth St.*
(p 119)

Best Swing Dancing
★ The Derby, *4500 Los Feliz Blvd.,*
at Hillhurst Ave. (p 122)

Best Supper Club
★★★ Largo, *432 N. Fairfax Ave.*
(p 123)

Best Biergarten
★ Red Lion Tavern, *2366 Glendale*
Blvd. (p 119)

Best Indie Rock
★★★ Spaceland, *1717 Silver Lake*
Blvd. (p 123)

Best Vodka Selection
★ Bar Lubitsch, *7702 Santa Monica*
Blvd. (p 118)

Best Waterbeds
★★ Standard Downtown, *550 S.*
Flower St. (p 122)

Best Fruity Cocktails with
Funny Names
★ Tiki-Ti, *4427 W. Sunset Blvd.*
(p 119); and ★★ Good Luck Bar,
1514 Hillhurst Ave. (p 119)

Women enjoying cocktails at the nightclub Area.

Beverly Hills & the Westside

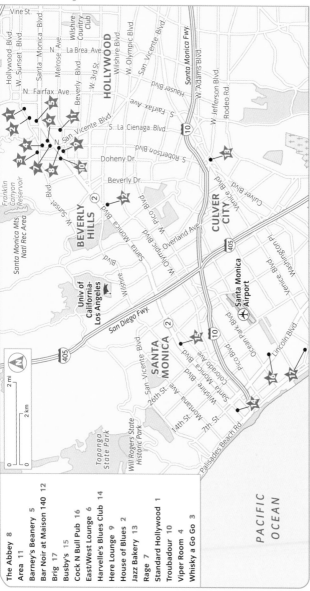

The Abbey 8
Area 11
Barney's Beanery 5
Bar Noir at Maison 140 12
Brig 17
Busby's 15
Cock N Bull Pub 16
East/West Lounge 6
Harvelle's Blues Club 14
Here Lounge 9
House of Blues 2
Jazz Bakery 13
Rage 7
Standard Hollywood 1
Troubadour 10
Viper Room 4
Whisky a Go Go 3

P 113: The world-famous Grauman's Chinese Theatre.

Hollywood

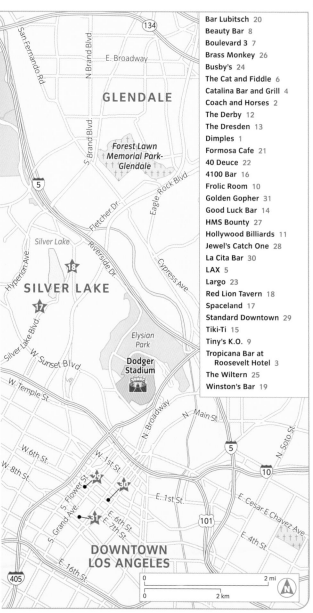

Nightlife A to Z

Bars & Pubs

★ **Bar Lubitsch** WEST HOLLY-WOOD This Russian-themed vodka parlor offers shadowy booths and 200 kinds of vodka for you and your comrades. *7702 Santa Monica Blvd., at Spaulding Ave.* ☎ *323/654-1234. Map p 116.*

★ **Beauty Bar** HOLLYWOOD On a bustling, barhopping block in Hollywood known as the "Cahuenga Corridor," this popular watering hole is fashioned after a mid-'60s salon, and offers manicures or henna tattoos along with pretty cocktails such as the Platinum Blonde. *1638 N. Cahuenga Blvd. (btwn Hollywood Blvd. & Selma Ave.).* ☎ *323/469-9440. www.beautybar.com. Map p 116.*

Brig VENICE A friendly, mixed crowd downs drinks in a hip and modern space with a DJ spinning on most nights. *1515 Abbot Kinney Blvd., at California Ave.* ☎ *310/399-7537. Map p 115.*

★ **The Cat and Fiddle** HOLLY-WOOD This English pub offers cheap pints during happy hour (Mon–Thurs 4–7pm), a garden

courtyard overflowing with ambience, and darts. *6530 W. Sunset Blvd. (btwn N. Highland Ave. & Vine St.).* ☎ *323/468-3800. www.the catandfiddle.com. Map p 116.*

★ **The Dresden** LOS FELIZ Check out the musical stylings of Marty and Elaine, the legendary lounge act you might remember from the movie *Swingers*. No cover, but it gets packed. *1760 N. Vermont Ave., at Kingswell Ave.* ☎ *323/665-4294. www.thedresden.com. Map p 116.*

★★★ **Formosa Café** WEST HOLLYWOOD Built in 1939 and declared a city landmark in 1991, this trolley car bar is perfect if you like your drinks dripping with nostalgia—Marilyn, Sinatra, and Elvis have all tippled here. *7156 Santa Monica Blvd., at Formosa Ave.* ☎ *323/ 850-9050. www.formosacafe.com. Map p 116.*

★★ **4100 Bar** SILVER LAKE Snake through the velvet curtain, and kick back in the red glow of the vaguely Asian decor. If you find a free nook or slouchy couch, take it—the place

The Formosa Café is a Hollywood landmark.

The bartender sports a dirndl dress at the Red Lion Tavern.

gets crowded. A giant Buddha statue chills in the corner. *4100 Sunset Blvd., at Manzanita St.* ☎ *323/666-4460. Map p 116.*

★ **Golden Gopher** DOWNTOWN This Downtown favorite is a long, dimly lit den with dark-wood walls, cozy booths, choice tunes, and, best of all, a tabletop Ms. Pac-Man game. The bar can also sell liquor "to go" due to some legal loophole dating back to 1905. If you dig the scene here, visit its sister bars: the Broadway Bar (830 Broadway) and Seven Grand (515 W. Seventh St.). *417 W. Eighth St., at S. Hill St.* ☎ *213/614-8001. www.goldengopherbar.com. Map p 116.*

★★ **Good Luck Bar** LOS FELIZ The room is a warm bath of kitsch, with Chinese decor played to the hilt: red dragons, paper lanterns, ornate ceiling tiles, and such. The bartenders are serious about their silly drinks—try a Yee Mee Koo. *1514 Hillhurst Ave., at W. Sunset Blvd.* ☎ *323/666-3524. www.goodluckbar.com. Map p 116.*

★ **Red Lion Tavern** SILVER LAKE Waitresses in dirndl dresses, an enviable collection of beer steins, sausage platters, and the largest assortment of German beers this side of München—*wunderbar!* *2366 Glendale Blvd., at Brier Ave.* ☎ *323/662-5337. www.redliontavern.net. Map p 116.*

★ **Tiki-Ti** LOS FELIZ Try the exotic cocktails—the Blood and Sand, the Great White Shark, Ray's Mistake—at what may be the world's tiniest tiki hut, serving loyal locals since 1961. *4427 W. Sunset Blvd., at Virgil Place.* ☎ *323/669-9381. www.tiki-ti.com. Map p 116.*

Winston's Bar WEST HOLLYWOOD Young Hollywood actors and agents booze and schmooze at this trendy ultralounge. No sign out front. *7746 Santa Monica Blvd., at N. Las Palmas Ave.* ☎ *323/654-0105. Map p 116.*

Dance Clubs
Area WEST HOLLYWOOD An open and airy dance floor with mod decor, this is where the young and fabulous get scandalous—*if* they can get beyond the velvet rope. Bottle service reservations, which are costly, are the only guaranteed way through the door. *643 N. La Cienega Ave. (btwn Melrose Ave. & Melrose Place).* ☎ *310/652-2012. www.sbeent.com. Cover $20. Map p 115.*

★ **Boulevard 3** HOLLYWOOD At the former Hollywood Athletic Club (established in 1924 with charter members such as Chaplin and

Go for a fruity cocktail at Tiki-Ti.

DeMille), this club offers a huge dance floor as well as a courtyard retreat with cozy cabanas. Call ahead for reservations, but you may still have to rely on the kindness of bouncers, if there is such a thing. *6523 W. Sunset Blvd., at N. Hudson Ave.* ☎ *323/466-2144. www.boulevard3.com. Cover $20. Map p 116.*

LAX HOLLYWOOD Club co-owner and former fiancé to Nicole Richie, DJ AM mans the turntables for his celebrity pals and anyone else lucky enough to get into the club styled like a groovy airport lounge. *1714 N. Las Palmas Ave., at Hollywood Blvd.* ☎ *323/464-0171. www.laxhollywood.com. Cover $20. Map p 116.*

Dive Bars

Coach and Horses HOLLYWOOD This down-and-dirty neighborhood bar is the antidote to the slick clubs along the Sunset Strip. This is not a place to see and be seen (it's too dark, anyway), but it's got attentive bartenders and a killer jukebox. Cash only. *7617 W. Sunset Blvd., at N. Curson Ave.* ☎ *323/876-6900. Map p 116.*

★ **Frolic Room** HOLLYWOOD Slumped next to the high-flying Pantages Theatre, this bar is refreshingly untouched by Hollywood's wave of regentrification. It's got an exuberant neon sign on the outside and a fading wallpaper mural of yesteryear celebrities on the inside. *6245 Hollywood Blvd., at Argyle Ave.* ☎ *323/462-5890. Map p 116.*

★ **HMS Bounty** KOREATOWN Attached to the lobby of the historic Gaylord apartment building, this bar has cheap drinks, a half-baked nautical theme, and waitresses who have seen it all, buster. Slide into the booth once favored by Jack "Just the facts, ma'am" Webb. *3357 Wilshire Blvd., at S. Kenmore Ave.* ☎ *213/385-7275. Map p 116.*

Tiny's K.O. HOLLYWOOD If you're looking for a beery hole-in-the-wall

The neon sign at Frolic Room.

Bar Noir at Maison 140.

with a punk-centric jukebox and oil paintings of clowns and topless broads, here ya go. *6377 Hollywood Blvd., at Cahuenga Blvd.* ☎ *323/462-9777. www.tinysko.com. Map p 116.*

Gay & Lesbian Bars & Clubs

The Abbey WEST HOLLYWOOD This indoor/outdoor cafe and bar has long been considered ground zero of West Hollywood's gay nightlife. Hunky bartenders serve up attitude and kicking cocktails to a friendly, mixed crowd. *692 N. Robertson Blvd., at Santa Monica Blvd.* ☎ *310/289-8410. www.abbeyfoodandbar.com. No cover. Map p 115.*

★ **East/West Lounge** WEST HOL-LYWOOD Gay professionals chill at this upscale club which serves specialty drinks (like puréed-fruit martinis) in a plush, conversation-friendly setting. On Tuesday nights, women have the floor. *801 Larrabee St., at Santa Monica Blvd.* ☎ *310/360-6186. www.eastwestlounge.com. No cover. Map p 115.*

Here Lounge WEST HOLLYWOOD This dance club is one of the few that have been successful mixing gays and lesbians. On Thursday and Friday nights, ladies strut their stuff. *696 N. Robertson Blvd., at Santa Monica Blvd.* ☎ *310/360-8455. www.herelounge.com. Cover $10. Map p 115.*

Jewel's Catch One MID-CITY This multiroom dance party started in 1972 as the nation's first black gay-and-lesbian disco, and most nights offers a mix of house, hip-hop, and salsa for ladies of all colors. *4067 W. Pico Blvd. (btwn Norton & 12th aves.).* ☎ *323/734-8849. www. jewelscatchone.com. Cover $10. Map p 116.*

Rage WEST HOLLYWOOD Each night has a different theme, but the basic formula is this: hot young men dancing. *8911 Santa Monica Blvd., at N. San Vicente Blvd.* ☎ *310/652-7055. www.ragewesthollywood.com. Cover $5–$15. Map p 115.*

Hotel Bars

★★★ **Bar Noir at Maison 140** BEVERLY HILLS This cozy hideaway dressed in black, white, and red is the perfect place for a romantic rendezvous. Try the Lady Godiva, their signature chocolatey-vodka drink. *140 S. Lasky Dr. (btwn Charleville & Wilshire blvds.).* ☎ *310/281-4000. www.maison140beverlyhills.com. Map p 115.*

★ **Standard Hollywood** WEST HOLLYWOOD The cobalt blue Astroturf surrounding the outdoor pool is packed with Hollywood's young groovers and shakers. The hipster drink du jour is a cold Colt 45 beer. *8300 W. Sunset Blvd., at N. Sweetzer Ave.* ☎ *323/650-9090. www.standardhotel.com. No cover. Map p 115.*

★★ Standard Downtown

DOWNTOWN   Plop onto the waterbed of a poolside red pod and drink in views of the twinkling skyscrapers. *550 S. Flower St. (btwn W. Fifth & W. Sixth sts.).* ☎ *213/892-8080. www.standardhotel.com. Cover $20 Fri & Sat nights & Sun afternoon. Map p 116.*

Tropicana Bar at Roosevelt Hotel

HOLLYWOOD   Although it's calmed down (thankfully) since its explosion onto the A-list party scene in 2005, this poolside bar with a mid-century, Palm Springs vibe is still a prime Hollywood see-and-be-seen locale. *7000 Hollywood Blvd., at N. Orange Dr.* ☎ *323/466-7000. www. hollywoodroosevelt.com. Map p 116.*

Karaoke

Brass Monkey

KOREATOWN   At this popular dive, the karaoke kicks off every night at 9pm, except Fridays when it starts at 4pm. The only trouble is choosing from 60,000 songs or, for first-timers, finding the door (on Mariposa, not Wilshire). *659 Mariposa Ave., at Wilshire Blvd.* ☎ *213/381-7047. www.caffebrass monkey.com. Cover $15 or 2-drink minimum. Map p 116.*

★ Dimples

BURBANK   This valley mainstay, which debuted in 1982, claims to be the first karaoke club in the western hemisphere. Your performance is projected on multiple screens, a video wall, cable-access, and the Internet. *3413 W. Olive Ave., at N. Lima St.* ☎ *818/842-2336. www.dimplesshowcase.com. Fri–Sat cover $5 after 10pm. Map p 116.*

Live Music & DJs

★ Catalina Bar and Grill

HOLLYWOOD   Cooking up classic jazz in Hollywood for 20 years, this 250-seat dinner club has hosted legends like Dizzy Gillespie, Art Blakey, and Wynton Marsalis. *6725 W. Sunset Blvd., at Highland Ave.* ☎ *323/466-2210. www.catalinajazzclub.com. Cover $10–$35. 2-drink or dinner minimum. Map p 116.*

★ The Derby

LOS FELIZ   This restaurant/nightclub/lounge offers a mix of local music, DJs, and stand-up comedy, but it made its reputation (with some help from the film *Swingers*) on its swing dancing on Sunday nights (lessons are offered 7–9pm). *4500 Los Feliz Blvd., at Hillhurst Ave.* ☎ *323/663-8979. www. clubderby.com. Cover $10. Map p 116.*

★★★ 40 Deuce

HOLLYWOOD   Ivan Kane's speak-easy-style club remains one of the hottest tickets in town, with classy-sexy dancers stripteasing to the sounds of a tight jazz combo. *5574 Melrose Ave., at N Gower St.* ☎ *323/465-4242. www. fortydeuce.com. Cover $10–$20. Map p 116.*

A dancer struts her stuff at 40 Deuce.

Harvelle's Blues Club SANTA MONICA   This dark, old-school nightclub presents authentic blues every night of the week. *1432 Fourth St., at Santa Monica Blvd.* ☎ *310/395-1676. www.harvelles.com. Cover $10. Map p 116.*

★ **House of Blues** HOLLYWOOD This slick, well-run venue hosts major acts from all genres. Try the Sunday gospel brunch, which serves up live gospel music and a buffet of Southern cuisine. *8430 W. Sunset Blvd., at N. Olive Dr.* ☎ *323/848-5100. www.hob.com. Cover $5 (in addition to ticket price). Tickets $20–$50. Map p 116.*

Jazz Bakery CULVER CITY   This no-frills, not-for-profit jazz venue presents live music 7 days a week. *3233 Helms Ave., at Venice Blvd.* ☎ *310/271-9039. www.jazzbakery. com. Cover $10–$30. Map p 116.*

★ **La Cita Bar** DOWNTOWN   Saturdays and Sundays offer authentic salsa and ranchera-style dancing, while the rest of the week, especially Thursday nights, presents DJs spinning for shimmying hipsters from Echo Park and Silver Lake. *336 S. Hill St., at W. Third St.* ☎ *213/687-7111. www.lacitabar.com. Thurs–Fri cover $5–$10. Map p 116.*

★★★ **Largo** WEST HOLLYWOOD This is a quiet, sit-down venue for acoustic sets (Eels, Fiona Apple) and comedic acts (Sarah Silverman, Patton Oswalt). Friday nights with producer/performer and musical mad scientist Jon Brion are legendary. *432 N. Fairfax Ave., btwn Oakwood & Rosewood aves.* ☎ *323/852-1073. www.largo-la.com. Cover $10. Map p 116.*

★★★ **Spaceland** SILVER LAKE Music experts with arty haircuts know this as the best stage to catch under-the-radar bands, many of whom—Beck, Foo Fighters, Arcade

A line forms outside the popular night spot Largo.

Fire—go on to the big leagues. *1717 Silver Lake Blvd., at Effie St.* ☎ *323/661-4380. www.clubspaceland.com. Cover $10. Map p 116.*

★★★ **Troubadour** WEST HOLLYWOOD   Opened in 1957, this club has played a vital role in the careers of Elton John, Tom Waits, Cheech and Chong, Guns N' Roses, and countless more. Today's lineup veers toward indie sensations like Clap Your Hands Say Yeah, the Fiery Furnaces, and Art Brut. *9081 Santa Monica Blvd., at N. Doheny Dr.* ☎ *310/276-6168. www.troubadour. com. Tickets $10–$15. Map p 115.*

Viper Room HOLLYWOOD   The small club, probably best known as the site of River Phoenix's death, packs a calendar full of up-and-coming rockers. Big names (Tom Petty, Pearl Jam) often drop in for surprise sets. *8852 W. Sunset Blvd., at Larrabee St.* ☎ *310/358-1880. www. viperroom.com. Tickets $10–$15. Map p 115.*

The legendary Whisky a Go Go on Sunset Boulevard.

★★ **Whisky a Go Go** HOLLY-WOOD   The legendary venue still presents a variety of musical acts, mostly hard rockin', including tribute bands to the greats that once played here: Led Zeppelin, Van Halen, and The Doors. *8901 W. Sunset Blvd., at N. San Vicente Blvd.* ☎ *310/652-4202. www.whiskyago go.com. Tickets $8–$40. Map p 115.*

★ **The Wiltern** MID–LOS ANGELES This Art Deco landmark presents popular indie acts (The Bravery, Ween, and Peter Bjorn and John) that have outgrown the Troubadour or Spaceland. *3790 Wilshire Blvd., at Western Ave.* ☎ *213/380-5005. www.wiltern.com. Tickets $55–$330. Map p 116.*

Sports Bars

★★★ **Barney's Beanery** WEST HOLLYWOOD   Its colorful movie and music history aside, this is an unpretentious place to catch a game, especially during the day. Choose from 132 types of beer. *8447 Santa Monica Blvd., at N. Olive Dr.* ☎ *323/654-2287. www.barneys beanery.com. Map p 115.*

★ **Busby's** HOLLYWOOD   Watch a game or two on the 50 flatscreen TVs, or test your skills at billiards, Ping-Pong, shuffle board, darts, or foosball. *5364 Wilshire Blvd., at Detroit St.* ☎ *323/525-5615. Also in Santa Monica at 3110 Santa Monica Blvd., at Berkeley St.* ☎ *310/828-4567. www.busbysonline.com. Map p 115.*

Cock N Bull Pub SANTA MONICA Big with sport fans and European expats, this Westside pub has TVs nearly always tuned to English soccer, and pitchers of Stella and Guinness. *2947 Lincoln Blvd., at Pier Ave.* ☎ *310/399-9696. Map p 115.*

★★ **Hollywood Billiards** HOLLY-WOOD   A cavernous, brick-walled space holds 40 well-kept Brunswick pool tables, 30 beers on tap, and eight big-screen TVs blasting sports. *5750 Hollywood Blvd. (btwn Wilton Place & N. Bronson Ave.).* ☎ *323/465-0115. www.hollywoodbilliards. com. Map p 116.* ●

Arts & Entertainment Best Bets

Best **Movie Theater for Cinephiles**
★★ ArcLight Cinemas, *6160 W. Sunset Blvd. (p 132)*

Best **Acoustics**
★★★ Walt Disney Concert Hall, *111 S. Grand Ave. (p 130)*

Best **Chance to Do the Wave**
★★ Dodger Stadium, *1000 Elysian Park Ave. (p 133)*

Best **Theater for a Hit Broadway Musical**
★★ Ahmanson Theater, *135 N. Grand Ave. (p 133);* and ★★ Pantages Theatre, *6233 Hollywood Blvd. (p 134)*

Best **Place to See an Opera**
★ Dorothy Chandler Pavilion, *135 N. Grand Ave. (p 130)*

Best **Old Hollywood Movie Experience**
★★★ Grauman's Chinese Theatre, *6925 Hollywood Blvd. (p 132)*

Best **Concert Under the Stars**
★★★ Hollywood Bowl, *2301 N. Highland Ave. (p 130)*

Best **Place to See David Beckham**
★ Home Depot Center, *1000 E. Victoria St. (p 133)*

Best **Pre-Show Cocktail**
★★ Geffen Playhouse, *10886 Le Conte Ave. (p 133)*

Best **Ongoing Saturday Night Live Auditions**
★★ Groundlings, *7307 Melrose Ave. (p 131)*

Best **Hip Comedy Scene**
★★ Largo, *432 N. Fairfax Ave. (Mon nights; p 131);* and ★★ M Bar and Restaurant, *1253 Vine St. (p 131)*

Best **Movie Theater for Kids**
★ El Capitan Theatre, *6838 Hollywood Blvd. (p 132)*

Best **Slam Dunk**
★★ Staples Center, *1111 S. Figueroa St. (p 133)*

A scene from David Mamet's Speed the Plow *at Geffen Playhouse.*

Hollywood

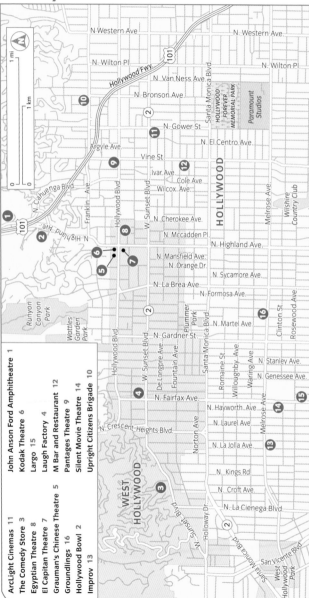

N Western Ave

N. Western Ave.

N. Wilton Pl.

N. Wilton Pl.

Hollywood Fwy

101

N. Van Ness Ave.

N. Bronson Ave.

Santa Monica Blvd

HOLLYWOOD FOREVER MEMORIAL PARK

Paramount Studios

N. Gower St

N. El Centro Ave.

Argyle Ave.

Vine St.

Ivar Ave.

Cole Ave.

Wilcox Ave.

HOLLYWOOD

Melrose Ave.

Wilshire Country Club

N. Cherokee Ave.

W. Sunset Blvd.

Hollywood Blvd

Franklin Ave.

N. Cahuenga Blvd

N. Highland Ave.

101

N. Mccadden Pl.

N. Highland Ave.

N. Mansfield Ave.

N. Orange Dr.

N. Sycamore Ave.

N. La Brea Ave.

N. Formosa Ave.

Runyon Canyon Park

Wattles Garden Park

Plummer Park

N. Martel Ave.

Clinton St.

Rosewood Ave.

Hollywood Blvd

W. Sunset Blvd

N. Gardner St.

Santa Monica Blvd.

Romaine St.

Willoughby Ave.

Waring Ave.

N. Stanley Ave.

N. Genessee Ave.

De Longpre Ave.

Fountain Ave.

N. Fairfax Ave.

N. Hayworth Ave.

N. Laurel Ave.

N. La Jolla Ave.

N. Crescent Heights Blvd.

Norton Ave.

Melrose Ave.

WEST HOLLYWOOD

N. Kings Rd.

N. Croft Ave.

N. La Cienega Blvd.

W. Sunset Blvd.

Holloway Dr.

Holloway Dr.

San Vicente Blvd.

West Hollywood Park

Santa Monica Blvd

1 mi

1 km

ArcLight Cinemas 11	John Anson Ford Amphitheatre 1
The Comedy Store 3	Kodak Theatre 6
Egyptian Theatre 8	Largo 15
El Capitan Theatre 7	Laugh Factory 4
Grauman's Chinese Theatre 5	M Bar and Restaurant 12
Groundlings 16	Pantages Theatre 9
Hollywood Bowl 2	Silent Movie Theatre 14
Improv 13	Upright Citizens Brigade 10

P 125: Performers at the Ford Amphitheatre.

Downtown

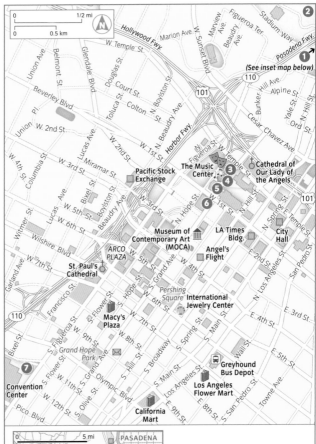

Ahmanson Theater **3**

Dodger Stadium **2**

Dorothy Chandler Pavilion **5**

Mark Taper Forum **4**

Pasadena Playhouse **1**

Staples Center **7**

Walt Disney Concert Hall **6**

Westwood

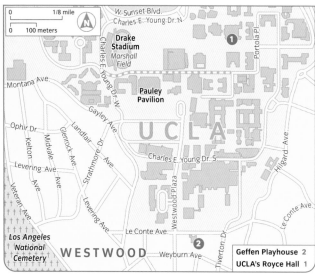

Geffen Playhouse 2
UCLA's Royce Hall 1

South Bay

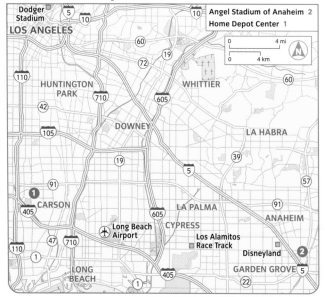

Angel Stadium of Anaheim 2
Home Depot Center 1

Arts & Entertainment A to Z

Classical Music, Opera & Dance

★ **Dorothy Chandler Pavilion**
DOWNTOWN   The massive auditorium is home to the nation's fourth-largest opera company, which continues to garner acclaim under the bold guidance of artistic director Plácido Domingo. Also, Dance at the Music Center hosts touring dance troupes such as the American Ballet Theatre. *135 N. Grand Ave., at Tom Bradley Blvd.* ☎ *213/972-8001 or 213/972-0711. www.musiccenter.org. Tickets $20–$220. Map p 128.*

★★★ **Hollywood Bowl** HOLLYWOOD   In 1922 the city's finest musicians, the Los Angeles Philharmonic, played the city's finest outdoor venue, the Hollywood Bowl. Thankfully, the tradition continues. Non-classical acts fill out the rest of the schedule. *2301 N. Highland Ave.* ☎ *323/850-2000. www.hollywoodbowl.com. Tickets $1–$147. Map p 127.*

John Anson Ford Amphitheatre HOLLYWOOD HILLS   For an outdoor amphitheater, this is an intimate setting—no seat is more than 96 feet away from the stage—to enjoy a diverse schedule of music, theater, and unique dance performances, such as a Bollywood take on *Alice in Wonderland. 2580 Cahuenga Blvd. East (near Hwy 101).* ☎ *323/461-3673. www.fordamphitheatre.org. Tickets $5–$75. Map p 127.*

U.C.L.A.'s Royce Hall WESTWOOD   Often likened to Carnegie Hall, this 1929 beauty has hosted performances by George Gershwin, Arnold Schoenberg, Ella Fitzgerald, Leonard Bernstein and the New York Philharmonic, Twyla Tharp, Frank Zappa, Mikhail Baryshnikov, and the Philip Glass Ensemble. *On the U.C.L.A. campus, 405 Hilgard Ave. (at Sunset Blvd.).* ☎ *310/825-2101. www.uclalive.org. Tickets $22–$100. Map p 129.*

★★★ **Walt Disney Concert Hall**
DOWNTOWN   Take any opportunity to attend a performance at this hall—a masterpiece for the eyes and ears. *111 S. Grand Ave., at First St.* ☎ *323/850-2000. www.laphil.com. Tickets $15–$142. Map p 128.*

The L.A. Opera performs Puccini's La Bohème *at Dorothy Chandler Pavilion.*

Royce Hall, on the U.C.L.A. campus.

Comedy

The Comedy Store HOLLYWOOD
Started in 1972 by Pauly Shore's
folks, this landmark club features
three separate rooms for funny business. Alumni include Richard Pryor,
John Belushi, David Letterman, Andy
Kaufman, Sam Kinison, and Gallagher.
*8433 W. Sunset Blvd., at Olive Dr.
☎ 323/650-6268. www.thecomedy
store.com. Tickets $10–$20, plus
2-drink minimum. Map p 127.*

★★ Groundlings HOLLYWOOD
For improv and sketch comedy in
L.A., nothing beats Groundlings,
whose long list of funny alumni
includes Will Ferrell, Lisa Kudrow,
Phil Hartman, Maya Rudolph, Jon
Lovitz, and Kathy Griffin. *7307 Melrose Ave., at Poinsettia Place.
☎ 323/934-4747. www.groundlings.
com. Tickets $6.25–$22. Map p 127.*

Improv WEST HOLLYWOOD At
some point in their careers, all the
big-time, stand-up comedians
have played Bud Friedman's club:
Steve Martin, Woody Allen, Robin
Williams, Jerry Seinfeld, Bill Cosby,
Jay Leno, Billy Crystal, Dana Carvey,
George Carlin, and Drew Carey.
8162 Melrose Ave., at N. Kilkea Dr.

☎ *323/651-2583. www.improv2.com.
Tickets $13–$18. Map p 127.*

★★ Largo HOLLYWOOD
Although known more for its excellent musical lineup, the supper club
features comedy on Monday nights
with names like Sarah Silverman,
Paul F. Tompkins, and Louis C.K. *432
N. Fairfax Ave., at Oakwood Ave.
☎ 323/852-1073. www.largo-la.
com. Cover varies; reservations recommended for dinner ($15 food
minimum). Map p 127.*

★ Laugh Factory HOLLYWOOD
Other than Michael "Kramer"
Richards's infamous meltdown in
2006, Jamie Masada's club has been
consistently bringing the funny
since 1979, when Richard Pryor
headlined the first show. Watch for
impromptu sets from Dave Chap-
pelle and Dane Cook. *8001 Sunset
Blvd., at Laurel Ave. ☎ 323/656-
1336. www.laughfactory.com. Tickets $20–$45. Map p 127.*

★★ M Bar and Restaurant
HOLLYWOOD Forget its minimall
location, and catch the cutting-
edge comedy—David Cross, Bob
Odenkirk, Patton Oswalt—at this

*Groundlings' impressive alumni include
comedian/actress Jennifer Coolidge.*

The El Capitan Theatre in Hollywood.

supper club with a speak-easy vibe. *1253 Vine St., at Fountain Ave.* ☎ *323/856-0036. www.mbar hollywood.com. Tickets $15 ($10 food minimum). Map p 127.*

Upright Citizens Brigade HOLLYWOOD The tiny theater rivals Groundlings for sketch-comedy supremacy, and the yuks per bucks ratio cannot be beat. *5919 Franklin Ave., at Bronson Ave.* ☎ *323/908-8702. www.ucbtheatre.com. Tickets $1–$8. Map p 127.*

Film
★★ ArcLight Cinemas HOLLYWOOD Reserved seating, audio that exceeds THX standards, a "black box" distraction-free design, and extra-wide seats with ample legroom—this is simply the most luxurious movie theater in town. *6160 W. Sunset Blvd., at Vine St.* ☎ *323/464-1478. www.arclightcinemas.com. Tickets $7.75–$14. Map p 127.*

★★ Egyptian Theatre HOLLYWOOD Home of the not-for-profit American Cinematheque, the historic showplace offers a program that dares to call film art: rare prints of 70mm classics, director retrospectives, film festivals, and in-person Q & A sessions with filmmakers and actors. *6712 Hollywood Blvd., at Las Palmas Ave.* ☎ *323/466-FILM. www.egyptiantheatre. com. Tickets $8–$10. Map p 127.*

★ El Capitan Theatre HOLLYWOOD Dancing Disney characters and a "Mighty Wurlitzer" pipe organ entertain the crowd before screenings of Disney/Pixar blockbusters at this historic theater, which hosted the world premiere of *Citizen Kane* in 1941. *6838 Hollywood Blvd., at Highland Ave.* ☎ *800/347-6396. Tickets $10–$22. Map p 127.*

★★★ Grauman's Chinese Theatre HOLLYWOOD Catch a flick at the most famous movie theater on the planet, unless it's closed off for a star-studded, red-carpet, flashbulb-popping premiere. *6925 Hollywood Blvd., at Highland Ave.* ☎ *323/464-8111. www.manntheatres.com. Tickets $8.25–$13. Map p 127.*

★ Silent Movie Theatre HOLLYWOOD A live organ accompanies the silent films of Buster Keaton, Charlie Chaplin, Greta Garbo, and Louise Brooks. *611 N. Fairfax Ave., at Clinton St.* ☎ *323/655-2520. www.silentmovietheatre.com. Tickets $10. Map p 127.*

Sports Venues

Angel Stadium of Anaheim

ANAHEIM   In 2002 the Los Angeles Angels clinched the World Series here on their home turf, a user-friendly venue that is actually accessible by public transportation. *2000 Gene Autry Way, at S. State College Blvd.* ☎ *888/796-HALO. www.angels. mlb.com. Tickets $5–$125. Map p 129.*

★★ kids Dodger Stadium DOWNTOWN

Built in 1962 to welcome the Dodgers from Brooklyn, this is one of Major League Baseball's classic stadiums, and currently the fifth oldest in use. *1000 Elysian Park Ave., at Stadium Way.* ☎ *866/DODGERS. www.dodgers.com. Tickets $6–$225. Map p 128.*

★ Home Depot Center CARSON

This 27,000-seat soccer-only stadium is the home field for both Chivas U.S.A. and the Los Angeles Galaxy, but good luck scoring tickets for the latter now that David Beckham captains the squad. *1000 E. Victoria St., at Tamcliff Ave.* ☎ *213/ 480-3232. www.homedepotcenter. com. Tickets $10–$250. Map p 129.*

Santa Anita Racetrack ARCADIA

Play the ponies at the oldest (established in 1934) and finest racetrack in southern California. Be sure to look for the statue of Seabiscuit, winner of the 1940 Santa Anita Handicap. *285 W. Huntington Dr., Arcadia.* ☎ *626/574-7223. www. santaanita.com. Admission $5–$20.*

★★ Staples Center DOWNTOWN

This state-of-the-art sporting palace plays home to the NHL's Los Angeles Kings, as well as the NBA's Los Angeles Clippers and Los Angeles Lakers. Enjoy some of the best celeb-spotting in town. *1111 S. Figueroa St., at 11th St.* ☎ *213/742-7300. www.staplescenter.com. Tickets $10–$275. Map p 128.*

Theaters

Actors' Gang CULVER CITY

Co-founded in 1982 by Tim Robbins, this experimental theater ensemble specializes in skewering the classics (Shakespeare, Ibsen, and Chekhov), garnering over 100 awards for their risk-taking productions. *9070 Venice Blvd., at Culver Blvd.* ☎ *310/838-4264. Tickets $25.*

★★ Ahmanson Theater DOWNTOWN

Enjoying the largest theatrical subscription base on the West Coast, the venue offers exclusive Los Angeles engagements of Tony Award–winning productions such as *Death of a Salesman, Who's Afraid of Virginia Woolf?, Doubt, Jersey Boys,* and *Avenue Q. 135 N. Grand Ave., at W. Temple St.* ☎ *213/628-2772. www.centerthe-atregroup.org. Tickets $20–$100. Map p 128.*

★★ Geffen Playhouse WESTWOOD

This striking venue near U.C.L.A. is known for showcasing film and television actors (Annette Bening, David Hyde Pierce) in their shuffling of classic works (Arthur Miller) with edgier fare (Terrence

David Beckham helps sell out the L.A. Galaxy soccer games played at the Home Depot Center.

Laurence Fishburne and Angela Bassett in a Pasadena Playhouse production of the August Wilson play Fences.

McNally, Wendy Wasserstein). *10886 Le Conte Ave., at Westwood Blvd.* ☎ *310/208-5454. www.geffen playhouse.com. Tickets $35–$110. Map p 129.*

Kirk Douglas Theatre CULVER CITY

This intimate 300-seat theater is an oft-overlooked member of the Center Theatre Group (which includes Ahmanson Theater and Mark Taper Forum) and tends to present more adventurous works such as a new musical fable by David Mamet. *9820 Washington Blvd., at Duquesne Ave.* ☎ *213/628-2772. Tickets $20–$40.*

★ Kodak Theatre HOLLYWOOD

This sparkling new home of the Academy Awards lends the Hollywood and Highland megaplex some much-needed street cred. The venue also hosts a variety of special events such as magic revues, book tours (J. K. Rowling), and musicals (Disney's *High School Musical*). *6801 Hollywood Blvd., at Highland Ave.* ☎ *323/308-6300. www.kodaktheatre.com. Tickets $23–$150. Map p 127.*

Mark Taper Forum DOWNTOWN

The intimate theater currently undergoes a $30-million overhaul, but will reopen in September 2008 with John Guare's *The House of Blue Leaves. 135 N. Grand Ave., at W. Temple St.* ☎ *213/628-2772. www. centertheatregroup.org. Map p 128.*

★★ Pantages Theatre HOLLY-WOOD

Home to the Academy Awards ceremony from 1949 to 1959, this lavishly restored Art Deco landmark presents hit Broadway musicals such as *The Lion King, The Producers,* and *Wicked. 6233 Hollywood Blvd., at Argyle Ave.* ☎ *323/468-1770. www.broadwayla.org. Tickets $81–$300. Map p 127.*

Pasadena Playhouse PASADENA

The historic theater, founded in 1917 and granted the title "State Theater of California" in 1937, has launched many Hollywood actors such as Raymond Burr, Gene Hackman, and Dustin Hoffman. *39 S. El Molino Ave., at E. Green St.* ☎ *626/356-7529. www.pasadenaplayhouse.org. Tickets $31–$60. Map p 128.* ●

Lodging Best Bets

Most **Luxurious**
★★★ Four Seasons Beverly Hills
$$$$ *300 S. Doheny Dr. (p 144)*

Most **Romantic**
★★★ Hotel Bel Air $$$$ *701 Stone Canyon Rd. (p 145)*

Best **Spot for Film Buffs**
★★★ Beverly Hills Hotel & Bungalows $$$$$ *9641 Sunset Blvd. (p 142)*

Best **Hip Budget Hotel**
Beverly Laurel Motor Hotel $
8010 Beverly Blvd. (p 142)

Best **Spot for Shopaholics**
★★ Beverly Wilshire $$$$$ *9500 Wilshire Blvd. (p 142)*

Best **Bed & Breakfast**
★ Bissell House Bed and Breakfast
$$ *201 Orange Grove Ave. (p 142)*

Most **Exclusive**
★★★ Chateau Marmont $$$$ *8221 Sunset Blvd. (p 143)*

Quirkiest **Decor**
★ Farmer's Daughter $$ *115 S. Fairfax Ave. (p 144)*

Most **Kid-Friendly**
★★ Loews Santa Monica Beach
$$$ *1700 Ocean Ave. (p 145)*

Best **Boutique Hotel**
★★★ Maison 140 $$ *140 S. Lasky Dr. (p 146)*

Most **Historic**
★★ Millennium Biltmore Hotel $$
506 S. Grand Ave. (p 146)

Best for **Business**
★★★ Raffles L'Ermitage $$$$$
9291 Burton Way (p 146)

Best **Sunday Brunch**
★★★ Ritz-Carlton Huntington
$$$$ *1401 S. Oak Knoll Ave. (p 147)*

Best **Views**
★★★ Shutters on the Beach $$$$
1 Pico Blvd. (p 147)

Hippest Hotel
★ Standard Hollywood $$ *8300 Sunset Blvd. (p 148);* and ★ Avalon Hotel $$$ *9400 W. Olympic Blvd. (p 141)*

Most **Rock 'n' Roll**
★★ Sunset Marquis Hotel & Villas
$$$ *1200 Alta Loma Rd. (p 148)*

Best **Hotel Bar**
★★ Viceroy Santa Monica $$$
1819 Ocean Ave. (p 148)

Best **Hotel Spa**
★★ W Los Angeles (Bliss Spa) $$$
930 Hilgard Ave. (p 148)

A luxurious room at the Four Seasons Beverly Hills.

Santa Monica & the Beaches

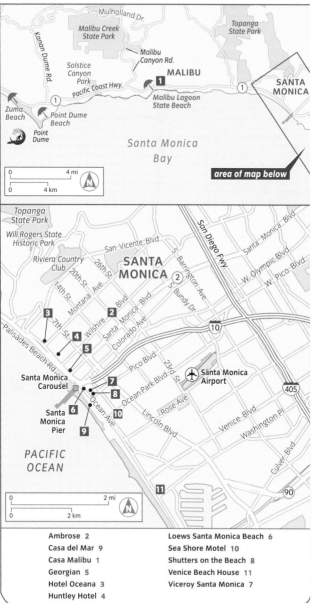

area of map below

Ambrose 2
Casa del Mar 9
Casa Malibu 1
Georgian 5
Hotel Oceana 3
Huntley Hotel 4

Loews Santa Monica Beach 6
Sea Shore Motel 10
Shutters on the Beach 8
Venice Beach House 11
Viceroy Santa Monica 7

P 135: The Casa del Mar in Santa Monica.

Beverly Hills & the Westside

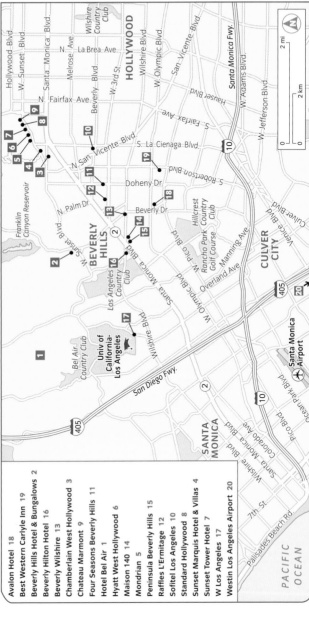

Hollywood

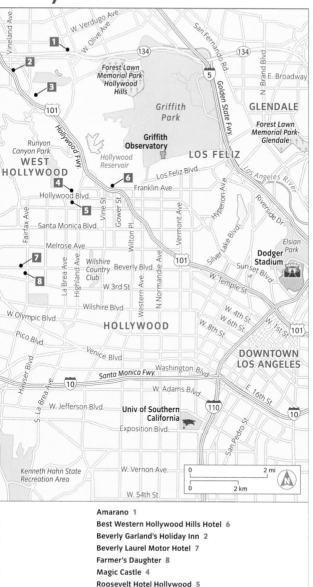

Amarano **1**
Best Western Hollywood Hills Hotel **6**
Beverly Garland's Holiday Inn **2**
Beverly Laurel Motor Hotel **7**
Farmer's Daughter **8**
Magic Castle **4**
Roosevelt Hotel Hollywood **5**
Sheraton Universal Hotel **3**

Downtown

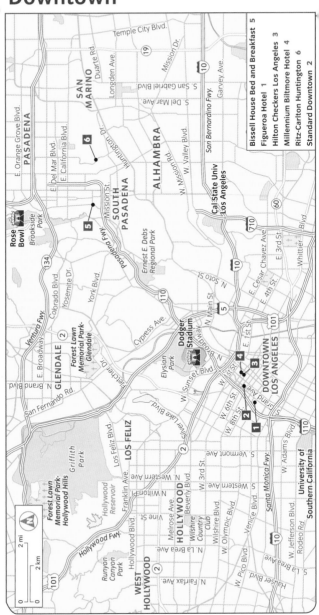

Bissell House Bed and Breakfast 5
Figueroa Hotel 1
Hilton Checkers Los Angeles 3
Millennium Biltmore Hotel 4
Ritz-Carlton Huntington 6
Standard Downtown 2

Lodging A to Z

Amarano BURBANK   This sleek boutique hotel is an excellent choice for valley accommodations. With a business center, meeting spaces, and high-speed Wi-Fi, it's especially appealing for guests who may be mixing business with pleasure. *322 N. Pass Ave. (btwn W. Oak & 134 Fwy.).* ☎ *818/842-8887. www.hotel amarano.com. 100 units. Doubles $185–$330. AE, DISC, MC, V. Map p 139.*

★ **Ambrose** SANTA MONICA This Asian-meets-Craftsman-style hotel sits in a quiet, residential Santa Monica neighborhood, and is a great choice for being close to, but not in the middle of, all the Westside action. Free breakfast includes choice pastries, fresh fruit, and organic yogurt. Other perks: free parking and Aveda bath products. *1255 20th St. (btwn Wilshire Blvd. & Arizona Ave.).* ☎ *310/315-1555. www.ambrose hotel.com. 77 units. Doubles $219–$249. AE, DISC, MC, V. Map p 137.*

★ **Avalon Hotel** BEVERLY HILLS Formerly the apartments of starlets such as Marilyn Monroe, the building has been redone in a winking '50s style with designer accessories (Charles Eames, George Nelson). The pool courtyard is a groovy scene; if you seek peace and quiet, ask for a room in the Canon building across the street. *9400 W. Olympic Blvd., at S. Canon Dr.* ☎ *310/277-5221. www. avalonbeverlyhills.com. 84 units. Doubles $279–$359. AE, DC, MC, V. Map p 138.*

Best Western Carlyle Inn BEVERLY HILLS   In a quiet neighborhood just south of Beverly Hills, this mall-like hotel offers comfy rooms with pleasant, if plain, decor. The full-breakfast buffet and sunny patios make this a good value. *1119 S. Robertson Blvd., at Whitworth Dr.* ☎ *310/275-4445. www.carlyle-inn. com. 32 units. Doubles $189–$239. AE, MC, V. Map p 138.*

★ **Best Western Hollywood Hills Hotel** HOLLYWOOD   All the contemporary-style rooms feature a fridge, a microwave, and wireless Internet. There's also a pool and the 101 Hills Coffee Shop, which is typically packed with hipsters. Hollywood is a short walk, and a Metro Line stop is 3 blocks away. *6141*

The pool at the Avalon Hotel.

Franklin Ave. (btwn N. Gower St. & Argyle Ave.). ☎ 323/464-5181. www.bestwesterncalifornia.com. 84 units. Doubles $149–$225. AE, DISC, MC, V. Map p 139.

kids Beverly Garland's Holiday Inn UNIVERSAL CITY   A pool, tennis courts, large grounds, free wireless, and a free shuttle to Universal Studios just down the street—this is a good option for families going to Universal, or for those who want to be close to freeway access. Speaking of, request a room toward Vineland Avenue for a bit more quiet. 4222 Vineland Ave., at Hwy. 101. ☎ 818/980-8000. www.beverly garland.com. 255 units. Doubles $159–$209. AE, MC, V. Map p 139.

★★★ Beverly Hills Hotel & Bungalows BEVERLY HILLS   The legendary "Pink Palace" opened in 1912 and still retains its golden-age glamour, ritziness, impeccable service, and that famous pink facade, which was immortalized on the cover of The Eagles' album Hotel California. 9641 Sunset Blvd., at Beverly Dr. ☎ 310/276-2251. www.thebeverly hillshotel.com. 204 units. Doubles $480–$590. AE, DC, DISC, MC, V. Map p 138.

The iconic sign of the Beverly Hills Hotel.

★ Beverly Hilton Hotel BEVERLY HILLS   The annual host of the Golden Globes has undergone an $80-million renovation and is looking more luxurious than ever. Great pool service. 9876 Wilshire Blvd., at Santa Monica Blvd. ☎ 310/274-7777. www.beverlyhilton.com. 570 units. Doubles $169–$350. AE, DC, DISC, MC, V. Map p 138.

Beverly Laurel Motor Hotel WEST HOLLYWOOD   If you can get past its worn appearance, you might dig this budget option with a great location and a kitschy, 1950s vibe. The clients are often scruffy, on-the-make actors and musicians, and the coffee shop downstairs, Swingers, rocks. 8010 Beverly Blvd., at N. Laurel Ave. ☎ 323/651-2441. 52 units. Doubles from $107. AE, DC, MC, V. Map p 139.

Beverly Wilshire BEVERLY HILLS   A $35-million renovation has spruced up this Four Seasons–managed hotel, which was originally built in 1928. The hotel restaurant is Wolfgang Puck's hit steakhouse, Cut. 9500 Wilshire Blvd., at Beverly Dr. ☎ 310/275-5200. www.fourseasons. com/beverlywilshire. 395 units. Doubles $495–$575. AE, DC, DISC, MC, V. Map p 138.

★ Bissell House Bed and Breakfast PASADENA   Set in a historic and architecturally rich neighborhood, this restored, antiques-filled Victorian built in 1887 is a comfy and cozy alternative to the typical L.A. hotel experience. 201 Orange Grove Ave., at Columbia St. ☎ 626/441-3535. www.bissell house.com. 5 units. Doubles $150–$225. AE, MC, V. Map p 140.

★★★ Casa del Mar SANTA MONICA   This resort hotel recaptures the glamour of its past as a 1920s beach club, with a rooftop pool and a sumptuous, velvet-draped lobby. Rooms offer ocean views, chaise

The eclectic and elegant lobby of the exclusive Chateau Marmont.

longues, and large, white-marble bathrooms with whirlpool tubs and Murad products. *1910 Ocean Way, at Pico Blvd.* ☎ *310/581-5533. www. hotelcasadelmar.com. 129 units. Doubles $405–$650. AE, DC, DISC, MC, V. Map p 137.*

★★ **kids Casa Malibu** MALIBU Book well in advance to snag these simple and clean beachfront digs that won't blow your budget. *22752 Pacific Coast Hwy., at Sweetwater Canyon Dr.* ☎ *310/456-2219. 21 units. Doubles $99–$249. AE, MC, V. Map p 137.*

★★ **Chamberlain West Hollywood** WEST HOLLYWOOD Converted from a 1970s apartment building, this chic boutique hotel offers large rooms with Hollywood Regency furniture and muted tones of blues and grays. On the rooftop lounge, a handsome crowd tans up before hitting the nearby clubs on Santa Monica Boulevard or the Sunset Strip. *1000 Westmount Dr., at Holloway Dr.* ☎ *310/657-7400. www.chamberlainwesthollywood. com. 112 units. Doubles $299–$339. AE, DC, MC, V. Map p 138.*

★★★ **Chateau Marmont** WEST HOLLYWOOD Built in 1927 to look like a Loire Valley castle, this landmark hotel has always prided itself on its exclusivity and privacy, which is why so many celebrities feel at home here. The rooms, suites, cottages, and bungalows are individually decorated (Gothic, Arts and Crafts, midcentury, Spanish), but all bask in the glow of Hollywood's golden era. *8221 Sunset Blvd., at Havenhurst Dr.* ☎ *323/656-1010. www.chateau marmont.com. 63 units. Doubles $350–$450. AE, DC, MC, V. Map p 138.*

★★ **kids Disney's Grand Californian Hotel & Spa** ANAHEIM If you're looking for luxury

For luxurious digs near Disneyland, book a room at Disney's Grand Californian Hotel & Spa.

The Best Lodging

Dark woods and warm colors characterize the rooms at the Figueroa Hotel.

accommodations near the Disneyland Resort, this is it. You may be surprised by the attention to detail in the Craftsman-style architecture and design. All rooms have views of the California Adventure park, and the kiddie pool (one of three pools) is shaped like Mickey Mouse. *1600 S. Disneyland Dr. (btwn W. Katella Ave. & W. Ball Rd.).* ☎ *714/635-2300. www.disneyland.com. 745 units. Doubles from $209. AE, DC, DISC, MC, V.*

★ **Farmer's Daughter** WEST HOLLYWOOD   You can't help but smile at this budget motel's crazy-cowpoke style: plaid curtains, denim bedspreads, thrift-store art, a recurring rooster motif, and a better-than-average supply of rusty pitchforks. And, boy, howdy—it's right across from the Farmers Market and CBS Television Center, where many guests try out for *The Price Is Right.* *115 S. Fairfax Ave., at W. First St.* ☎ *323/937-3930. www.farmers daughterhotel.com. 66 units. Doubles $115–$135. AE, DISC, MC, V. Map p 139.*

★★ **Figueroa Hotel** DOWNTOWN   Downtown adventurers might enjoy this moderately priced hotel with eclectic, exotic decor such as Moroccan chandeliers, Indian fabrics, Mexican tiles, and hand-woven Afghani kilims. A pool and patio bar complete the urban oasis. *939 S. Figueroa St., at Olympic Blvd.* ☎ *213/627-8971. www.figueroahotel.com. 285 units. Doubles $104–$134. AE, DC, MC, V. Map p 140.*

★★★ **Four Seasons Beverly Hills** BEVERLY HILLS   Fabulousness and impeccable service in the heart of Beverly Hills—this is for those who are living the dream, baby. *300 S. Doheny Dr., at Burton Way.* ☎ *800/332-3442. www.fourseasons. com/beverlyhills. 285 units. Doubles $395–$475. AE, DC, DISC, MC, V. Map p 138.*

★ **Georgian** SANTA MONICA   This Art Deco masterpiece facing Santa Monica beach combines a lot of luxury and bit of history—during

Kick back and relax at the pool at the Four Seasons Beverly Hills.

The ultramodern lobby of the Huntley Hotel.

Prohibition Bugsy Siegel opened a speak-easy in the hotel's basement. *1415 Ocean Ave. (btwn Santa Monica Blvd. & Broadway).* ☎ *800/538-8147 or 310/395-9945. www.georgian hotel.com. 84 units. Doubles $235–$275. AE, DC, DISC, MC, V. Map p 137.*

★ **Hilton Checkers Los Angeles** DOWNTOWN In a historic building from 1927, this perfectly serviceable hotel may not have the scene or the swankiness of other Downtown options, but you can sometimes get a great rate online. *535 S. Grand Ave. (btwn Fifth & Sixth sts.).* ☎ *213/624-1000. www.hiltoncheckers.com. 188 units. Doubles $149–$299. AE, DC, DISC, MC, V. Map p 140.*

★★★ **Hotel Bel Air** BEL AIR The stunning grounds set this legend apart from other luxury hotels in L.A. Pink stucco buildings are nestled among 12 lush acres with manicured gardens, canopies of bougainvillea, old-as-dirt sycamores and live oaks, a koi pond, a swan lake, and fragrant flowers. *701 Stone Canyon Rd., north of Sunset Blvd.* ☎ *800/648-4097 or 310/472-1211. www.hotelbelair.com. 91 units. Doubles $395–$625. AE, DC, DISC, MC, V. Map p 138.*

★★ **Hotel Oceana** SANTA MONICA This hotel offers an oceanfront location, luxury amenities, bright decor, and huge suites, which make it a good fit for families or shares. *849 Ocean Ave., at Montana Ave.* ☎ *310/393-0486. www.hoteloceana santamonica.com. 63 units. Doubles $380–$500. AE, DC, DISC, MC, V. Map p 137.*

★★ **Huntley Hotel** SANTA MONICA Bed down in postmodern coolness at this hotel close to the beach and prime Santa Monica shopping. It may be worth a stay just to score a white-leather seat at the white-hot bar, The Penthouse. *1111 Second St., at California Ave.* ☎ *310/394-5454. www.thehuntleyhotel.com. 209 units. Doubles $319–$449. AE, DC, DISC, MC, V. Map p 137.*

★ **Hyatt West Hollywood** WEST HOLLYWOOD This is the infamous "Riot Hyatt" where rock 'n' roll will never die . . . although it will get older, with more sedate decor and better amenities. Avoid the rooms on lower floors facing the street. *8401 Sunset Blvd., at Kings Rd.* ☎ *800/233-1234 or 323/656-1234. www.westhollywood. hyatt.com. 262 units. Doubles $129–$245. AE, DC, DISC, MC, V. Map p 138.*

★★ **kids Loews Santa Monica Beach** SANTA MONICA Kids and pets receive welcome gifts at check-in, and adults will love the palm tree–lined lobby, ocean views, heated pool, spa and fitness center, and easy access to Santa Monica

Pier and Third Street Promenade. *1700 Ocean Ave., at Colorado Ave.* ☎ *800/235-6397 or 310/458-6700. www.loewshotels.com. 340 units. Doubles $305–$460. AE, DC, DISC, MC, V. Map p 137.*

Magic Castle HOLLYWOOD Walkable to Hollywood Boulevard and a Red Line stop, this apartment complex–turned–motel offers large, sparsely designed rooms, most with fully equipped kitchens. *7025 Franklin Ave. (btwn Highland & La Brea aves.).* ☎ *800/741-4915 or 323/851-0800. www.magiccastle hotel.com. 49 units. Doubles $129. AE, DC, DISC, MC, V. Map p 139.*

★★★ Maison 140 BEVERLY HILLS Originally a boarding house owned by Lillian Gish, this superchic boutique hotel blends elements that are French, Far East, and far out. Stroll Rodeo Drive nearby, and then cozy up in the dark and velvety Bar Noir, the trystiest hotel bar around. *140 S. Lasky Dr. (btwn Wilshire & Charleville blvds.).* ☎ *800/670-6182 or 310/281-4000. www.maison140beverlyhills. com. 43 units. Doubles $229–$289. AE, DC, MC, V. Map p 138.*

A guest room at Maison 140.

★★ Millennium Biltmore Hotel DOWNTOWN   Architecture lovers should consider a stay at this 1923 historic landmark for its stunning lobby, halls, and ballrooms, which have been used for Oscar® ceremonies, JFK's 1960 DNC headquarters, and, of course, movie locations *(Ghostbusters, Beverly Hills Cop).* However, the rooms, while elegant, are rather small. *506 S. Grand Ave., at W. Fifth St.* ☎ *213/624-1011. www.millenniumhotels.com. 683 units. Doubles $130–$330. AE, DC, DISC, MC, V. Map p 140.*

Mondrian WEST HOLLYWOOD This stylish white-on-white high rise is best known for its poolside bar, the exclusive Skybar, which has made a recent resurgence as a celebrity hot spot. A $20-million renovation promises a complete overhaul of all the rooms. *8440 W. Sunset Blvd., at Queens Rd.* ☎ *800/606-6090 or 323/650-8999. www.mondrianhotel. com. 237 units. Doubles $310–$560. AE, DC, DISC, MC, V. Map p 138.*

★★★ Peninsula Beverly Hills BEVERLY HILLS   You'll get an opulent, European-styled room and flawless service if you can fork out the cash to stay at this gardenlike oasis. A lavish spa covers 42,000 square feet. *9882 S. Santa Monica Blvd., at Wilshire Blvd.* ☎ *800/462-7899 or 310/551-2888. www.peninsula.com. 196 units. Doubles $395–$525. AE, DC, DISC, MC, V. Map p 138.*

★★★ Raffles L'Ermitage BEVERLY HILLS   The Asian-influenced rooms are huge and serene, with work desks that are actually for working, and technological perks like free Wi-Fi, multiple phone lines, 40-inch flatscreen TVs, and bedside controls for lighting and climate. The rooftop pool area boasts 360-degree views of the city and mountains. *9291 Burton Way, at N. Foothill Rd.* ☎ *800/800-2113 or 310/278-3344.*

find a real bargain. The low-rise motel may look humdrum, but the rooms are spacious and superclean, with tile floors and granite countertops. *2637 Main St., at Ocean Park Blvd.* ☎ *310/392-2787. www.seashore motel.com. 24 units. Doubles $75–$95. AE, DISC, MC, V. Map p 137.*

★ kids **Sheraton Universal Hotel** UNIVERSAL STUDIOS Convenience and location make this a popular choice for families eager to hit Universal Studios, Warner Brothers Studios, or Hollywood. *333 Universal Hollywood Dr., at Lankershim Blvd.* ☎ *800/325-3535 or 818/980-1212. www.sheraton.com/universal. 436 units. Doubles $149–$219. AE, DC, DISC, MC, V. Map p 139.*

★★★ **Shutters on the Beach** SANTA MONICA This shingled building on the sand combines the luxury of a fine hotel with the breeziness of a beach cottage. Watch the sun set on the ocean from your own private balcony. *1 Pico Blvd., at Neilson Way.* ☎ *800/334-9000 or 310/458-0030. www.shuttersonthebeach.com. 198 units. Doubles $405–$650. AE, DC, DISC, MC, V. Map p 137.*

★ **Sofitel Los Angeles** WEST HOLLYWOOD This hotel offers understated European elegance and easy access to oodles of shopping— Beverly Center, Third Street, Robertson Boulevard. Slip into the hotel's trendy Stone Rose Lounge for a late-night martini. Pet friendly. *8555 Beverly Blvd., at La Cienega Ave.* ☎ *310/278-5444. www.sofitel.com. 295 units. Doubles $309–$349. AE, DC, DISC, MC, V. Map p 138.*

★★ **Standard Downtown** DOWNTOWN Accommodations are cheeky and modern, but you come here to groove at the retro-style rooftop pool and bar, a sensation since debuting in 2002. *550 S. Flower St. (btwn W. Fifth & W. Sixth sts.).*

The Ritz-Carlton Huntington in Pasadena.

www.raffles.com. 119 units. Doubles $438. AE, DC, DISC, MC, V. Map p 138.

★★★ **Ritz-Carlton Huntington** PASADENA Set on 23 acres of lush gardens in the foothills of San Gabriel mountains, this beautiful hotel, built in 1906, makes a great base for exploring Downtown, as well as the museums and architectural homes of Pasadena. The Terrace Restaurant offers a wonderful, relaxed Sunday brunch. *1401 S. Oak Knoll Ave., at Hillcrest Ave.* ☎ *800/241-3333 or 626/568-3900. www.ritzcarlton.com. 392 units. Doubles $279–$399. AE, DC, MC, V. Map p 140.*

★★ **Roosevelt Hotel Hollywood** HOLLYWOOD This hotel, site of the first Academy Awards in 1929, has been restored to its former glory—just ask the ghost of Montgomery Clift, who they say still haunts the building. *7000 Hollywood Blvd., at N. Orange Dr.* ☎ *800/950-7667 or 323/466-7000. www.hollywoodroosevelt.com. 302 units. Doubles $189–$299. AE, DC, DISC, MC, V. Map p 139.*

★ **Sea Shore Motel** SANTA MONICA Among the chichi shops on Santa Monica's Main Street, you can

☎ 213/892-8080. www.standard hotel.com. 205 units. Doubles from $185. AE, DC, DISC, MC, V. Map p 140.

★ **Standard Hollywood** HOLLYWOOD   The vibe is "motel as pop art." In the lobby you'll find bubble chairs dangling over shag carpeting, beanbag pod chairs, and a hot chick lounging in a glass display behind the check-in desk. Rooms can get loud when a party's pumping poolside, which is nearly always. *8300 Sunset Blvd., at Sweetzer Ave.* ☎ 323/650-9090. www.standardhotel.com. 139 units. Doubles $109–$235. AE, DC, DISC, MC, V. Map p 138.

★★ **Sunset Marquis Hotel & Villas** WEST HOLLYWOOD   A Mediterranean oasis off the Sunset Strip, this all-suite hotel has long catered to the high-profile musician crowd (Stones, U2, Eminem); there's even a state-of-the-art recording studio in the basement. The Whiskey Bar is impossible to get into, unless you're a hotel guest or you're famous or both. *1200 Alta Loma Rd. (btwn Sunset Blvd. & Halloway Dr.).* ☎ 310/657-1333. www.sunsetmarquishotel. com. 114 units. Doubles $299–$355. AE, DC, DISC, MC, V. Map p 138.

Sunset Tower Hotel WEST HOLLYWOOD   A 1929 Art Deco landmark that has seen tenants such as Frank Sinatra, Marilyn Monroe, and Howard Hughes, this hotel takes a straight-faced look back at Hollywood's heyday, and presents a grownup's version of the Sunset Strip. Rooms have views, comfortable beds, and Kiehl's toiletries. *8358 W. Sunset Blvd. (btwn Crescent Heights & La Cienega blvds.).* ☎ 323/654-7100. www.sunsettower hotel.com. 74 units. Doubles from $269. AE, DISC, MC, V. Map p 138.

★ **Venice Beach House** VENICE   No designer decor, no high-end amenities, but most importantly, no attitude—this warm and charming B&B occupies a historic Craftsman bungalow just a block from Venice Beach. Half of the rooms have private bathrooms. *15 30th Ave., at Speedway.* ☎ 310/823-1966. www. venicebeachhouse.com. 9 units (5 w/private bathroom). Doubles $145–$235. AE, MC, V. Map p 137.

★★ **Viceroy Santa Monica** SANTA MONICA   This glamorous retreat features what I'd call Groovy Colonialism decor, and two outdoor pools with swank cabanas. The rooms have high-speed Internet, flatscreen TVs, luxury linens, and marble baths with Molton Brown products. Pet friendly. *1819 Ocean Ave., at Pico Blvd.* ☎ 800/670-6185 or 310/260-7500. www.viceroysantamonica.com. 170 units. Doubles $299–$389. AE, DC, DISC, MC, V. Map p 137.

★★ **W Los Angeles** WESTWOOD   This sleek, all-suite hotel near U.C.L.A. makes a good base for exploring the Westside. It offers a relaxing pool, and a bustling bar called Whiskey Blue. Pet friendly. *930 Hilgard Ave., at Le Conte Ave.* ☎ 800/W-HOTELS or 310/208-8765. www.starwood.com/ whotels. 258 units. Doubles from $299. AE, DC, DISC, MC, V. Map p 138.

★ **Westin Los Angeles Airport** AIRPORT   Corporate-style convenience with Westin's signature Heavenly Bed. *5400 W. Century Blvd., at Concourse Way.* ☎ 800/937-8461 or 310/216-5858. www.westin.com/los angelesairport. 740 units. Doubles $160–$299. AE, DC, DISC, MC, V. Map p 138. ●

A guest room at the W Los Angeles.

Disneyland Resort

Ball Rd.

Santa Ana Fwy.

Mickey & Friends Parking

Pinocchio Parking

W. Magic Way

Dowtown Disney Parking

Valet Parking

Disneyland Dr.

DISNEYLAND

Anaheim Resort Public Transportation Center

Disneyland Hotel Taxi Stand

Harbor Blvd.

MAIN ENTRY PLAZA

East Shuttle Area

Ticketing

DOWNTOWN DISNEY

DISNEY'S GRAND CALIFORNIAN HOTEL

DISNEY'S PARADISE PIER HOTEL

CALIFORNIA ADVENTURE

Guest Drop-off

Timon Parking

Katella Ave.

Anaheim Convention Center

1 Main Street U.S.A.
2 Sleeping Beauty Castle
3 Finding Nemo Submarine Voyage
4 Space Mountain
5 Pirates of the Caribbean
6 Toontown
7 Ralph Brennan's Jazz Kitchen Express

8 Soarin' Over California
9 Grizzly River Run
10 California Screamin'
11 Maliboomer
12 Mulholland Madness
13 Twilight Zone Tower of Terror

Previous page: Grapes on the vine in the Santa Ynez Wine Country.

The resort is a combination of ★★★ **Disneyland** (the iconic amusement park that Uncle Walt unveiled in 1955), ★★ **Disney California Adventure** (a thrill-driven theme park built in 2001 as a sanitized, scaled-down version of the Golden State), three Disney hotels, and Downtown Disney (a shopping, eating, and entertainment complex that connects everything). *1313 S. Harbor Blvd., Anaheim.* ☎ *714/781-4565. www.disney.com. 1-day Theme Park: $63 adults & children 10 & up, $53 children 3–9, free for children 2 & under. 1-day Park Hopper: $83 adults & children 10 & up, $73 children 3–9. Multiday passes offer substantial discounts.*

1 Main Street USA. An idealization of small-town America at the turn of the 20th century, Main Street takes you back to an innocent time of ice-cream parlors, barber-shop quartets, horse-drawn trolleys, and shiny fire engines. Above the firehouse (but not available to the public) is the room where Walt often stayed during the park's construction; it remains fully furnished with a lamp in the front window that shines eternally as a tribute. *Entrance, Disneyland.*

2 Sleeping Beauty Castle. Modeled after the Neuschwanstein royal palace in Bavaria, the turreted, 77-foot-tall castle appears even grander due to the forced perspective of its architecture, which tricks the eye, especially from a distance. One of the spires is deliberately missing a small patch of gold-leaf, per instructions from Walt, who never wanted to think of the park as complete. The castle is one of the park's original 17 attractions. *Entrance to Fantasyland, Disneyland.*

3 Finding Nemo Submarine Voyage. This latest attraction in Tomorrowland replaces the old Submarine Voyage which was based on *20,000 Leagues Under the Sea* (featuring Captain Nemo, by the

The grand, turreted castle marks the entrance to Fantasyland at Disneyland.

Need to cool off? Head straight for Grizzly River Run.

way, and written by futurist Jules Verne, who inspired much of the look of Tomorrowland). Through the portal of a bright yellow submarine, you'll see Nemo and his pals swimming in the sea. You can also listen to the action with "sonar hydrophones." *Tomorrowland, Disneyland.*

4 Space Mountain. The pitch blackness of outer space denies the power of sight, but the roller coaster is an assault on the rest of your senses. Since 1977 this has been Disneyland's most adrenaline-pumping ride. *Tomorrowland, Disneyland.*

5 Pirates of the Caribbean. With the success of the three *Pirates of the Caribbean* movies, the ride has been updated to include new special effects, story elements, voices, and an Audio-Animatronics figure of Johnny Depp's character, Captain Jack Sparrow. Thankfully, the off-putting display of lascivious pirates chasing "wenches" has been cut. *New Orleans Sq., Disneyland.*

6 Toontown. This part of the park is meant to look like you

tripped into a cartoon—everything is bright and poofy, and you can't find a straight line (or a straight face) anywhere. Little kids love meeting Mickey or Goofy, and romping around the playground. *Toontown, Disneyland.*

7 Ralph Brennan's Jazz Kitchen Express. If you need a pit stop between the two parks, there are snack options aplenty in Downtown Disney. My favorite is the Big Easy–themed Jazz Kitchen, where you can pick up coffee, beignets, or Cajun-style po' boys. *1590 S. Disneyland Dr., Downtown Disney.* ☎ *714/776-5200. $.*

8 Soarin' Over California. Rush over to this virtual ride with the real lines and use your FAST-PASS for this state-of-the-art simulation of a hang-glider ride over the best parts of the state. Wheeee, there's Yosemite! *Condor Flats, Golden State, Disney's California Adventure.*

9 Grizzly River Run. Every amusement park needs a ride to

How to Conquer (& Enjoy) Disneyland

The parks can get extremely crowded during the summer, especially on weekends and holidays. Here are a few coping strategies: (1) use a **FASTPASS** at popular rides with long lines—look for the FASTPASS machines near the entrance of an attraction and "check in" with your ticket, receive a voucher with a time slot (say, an hour or two later), and return to the head of the line at the designated time; (2) purchase tickets in advance on the website; (3) do your research ahead of time—know which attractions you want to see most; (4) arrive a half-hour before the gates open; (5) go against the grain—take advantage during mealtimes or parades when lines may be shorter; and (6) remember, you're having fun.

cool you down on a hot day, right? This white-water-raft trip around Grizzly Peak—the bear-shaped mountain is the park's centerpiece—splashes through mine shafts and caves before dropping your raft down a geyser-filled gorge. *Grizzly Peak Recreation Area, Golden State, Disney's California Adventure.*

🔟 **California Screamin'.** Paradise Pier evokes the great beachfront amusement parks of yesteryear such as Santa Monica or Venice. This classic roller coaster, one of the fastest rides in either park, does a vertical loop along the outline of Mickey's head. *Paradise Pier, Disney's California Adventure.*

⓫ **Maliboomer.** Mimicking those ring-a-bell, sledgehammer tests of strength found at carnivals, this ride slingshots you nearly 200 feet into the air in 4 seconds. For a brief moment 18 stories high, you'll experience zero gravity. I recommend that you try this one *before* you eat. *Paradise Pier, Disney's California Adventure.*

⓬ **Mulholland Madness.** This "wild mouse" roller coaster is a

wacky take on one of L.A.'s most famous drives. Make sure your child is comfortable with a few unexpected drops and turns. *Paradise Pier, Disney's California Adventure.*

⓭ **Twilight Zone Tower of Terror.** Would you like to plummet down an abandoned elevator shaft in the creepy Hollywood Tower Hotel, the tallest building in the entire resort? The Twilight Zone tidbits make the build-up excrutiatingly tense. *Hollywood Pictures Backlot, California Adventure.*

Thrill-seekers will love the Twilight Zone Tower of Terror.

Santa Barbara

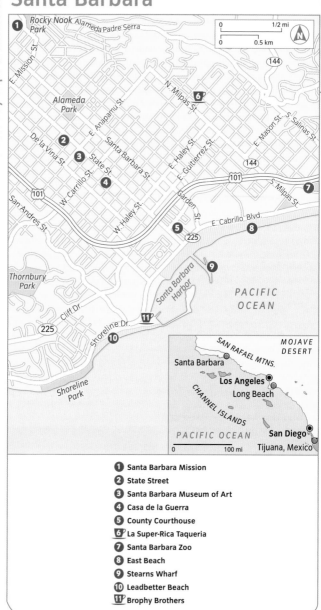

1 Santa Barbara Mission
2 State Street
3 Santa Barbara Museum of Art
4 Casa de la Guerra
5 County Courthouse
6 La Super-Rica Taqueria
7 Santa Barbara Zoo
8 East Beach
9 Stearns Wharf
10 Leadbetter Beach
11 Brophy Brothers

The rugged Santa Ynez Mountains to the north, the sparkling Pacific Ocean to the south, harmonious Spanish Mission–Revival architecture, and a Mediterranean climate—Santa Barbara more than lives up to its billing as the "American Riviera." A hundred miles north of Los Angeles, the exclusive enclave is home to many a mega-celebrity: Oprah Winfrey, Tom Cruise and family, Steve Martin, Kevin Costner, and Michael Douglas.

1 Santa Barbara Mission. With its stately, pink sandstone facade and twin bell towers, the aptly nicknamed "Queen of the Missions" occupies a verdant hill overlooking the town and the Channel Islands in the distance. The Spanish Franciscans established the mission in 1786 using the labor and craftsmanship of native Chumash Indians (whom they were trying to convert). Over the years, the original adobe buildings have seen substantial additions and renovations— earthquakes in 1812 and 1925 caused serious damage. Take the self-guided tour or relax in the quiet courtyard. *2201 Laguna St. (at Los Olivos St.), Santa Barbara.* ☎ *805/682-4149. www.sbmission.org. Daily 9am–5pm. $4 adults, free for children under 12.*

2 State Street. This is the town's main drag with restaurants, bars, movie theaters, art galleries, and countless shops—everything from souvenir trinkets to high-end fashion. *State St. (from Victoria St. to the beach).*

3 Santa Barbara Museum of Art. The small but excellent museum boasts an eclectic permanent collection featuring classical antiquities, 19th- and 20th-century paintings, contemporary Latin American Art, photography, and most impressively, Asian art from India, Tibet, China, Japan, and southeast Asia. *1130 State St., Santa Barbara.* ☎ *805/963-4364. www.sbmuseart.org. $9 adults, $7 seniors, $6 students & children 6–17, free for children under 6. Free for everyone on Thurs & the 1st Sun of the month.*

The Santa Barbara Museum of Art.

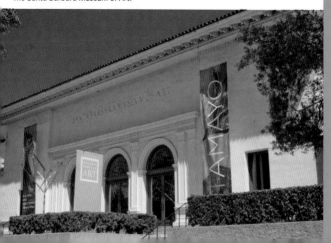

For sublime views of the surrounding area, ascend the 85-foot clock tower of the County Courthouse.

4 Casa de la Guerra. It's all too easy to overlook this city and state landmark located just off State Street near the Paseo Nuevo mall. The adobe home was built in the 1820s by the fifth Presidio comandante, José de la Guerra. Following the city's devastating earthquake in 1925, the Casa served as a model of style and architecture for the city's rebuilding process. If you enjoy the antiques and artifacts here, continue on a few blocks to El Presidio de Santa Barbara at 123 E. Canon Perdido St. *15 E. De la Guerra St., Santa Barbara.* ☎ *805/966-6961. Thurs–Sun noon–4pm. $3 adults, free for children under 17.*

5 ★ County Courthouse. This National Historic Landmark is sometimes called the most beautiful government building in America. Built in 1929 in the Spanish-Moorish style, it features a grand archway, turrets, wrought-iron balconies, mosaic tiles, hand-carved doors, hand-painted ceilings, striking murals that illustrate the history of the land, and a grassy sunken garden. At the top of the 85-foot "El Mirador" clock tower, you can admire gorgeous views of the mountains, coastline, and the red-tile roofs of the historic section. *100 Anacapa St., Santa Barbara.* ☎ *805/962-6464. Free admission. Free guided tours Mon–Tues & Fri at 10:30am, Mon–Sat at 2pm.*

6 La Super-Rica Taqueria. Rarely do little *taquerias* create this much hoopla. Blame it on Julia Childs, who used to queue up for her favorite tacos in town. Authentic, spicy, and cheap—everything is delicious, so feel free to gamble on the daily specials even if you trip on the pronunciation. *622 N. Milpas St., Santa Barbara.* ☎ *805/963-4940. Cash only. $.*

7 kids Santa Barbara Zoo. Considered one of the best small zoos in the country, this zoo presents 500 animals on 30 acres of botanic gardens overlooking the Pacific Ocean. Exhibits include several endangered species such as Asian elephants, snow leopards, lemurs, white-handed gibbons, and the largest of all the primates, the western lowland gorillas. One of the zoo's most popular creatures is Gemina, a giraffe with a crooked neck (odd looking, maybe, but perfectly healthy). *500 Niños Dr., Santa Barbara.* ☎ *805/962-5339. www.santabarbarazoo.org. Daily 10am–5pm. $10 adults, $8 children 2–12, free seniors & children under 2.*

⑧ **East Beach.** A wide, sandy beach with volleyball courts, Rollerblading path, picnic areas, playground, and restrooms, all hemmed in by a green lawn—this could be Santa Barbara's best all-around beach. It's also one of the most accessible, across from the zoo and stretching to the pier. *East of Stearns Wharf. Sunrise–10pm.*

⑨ **Stearns Wharf.** The oldest working wharf in California is located at the very bottom of State Street (look for the statue of three dolphins), and pulls in five million visitors a year. Eat, shop, go fishing, or try the Ty Warner Sea Center, full of kid-friendly interactive exhibits on marine education. *End of State St., Santa Barbara.*

⑩ **Leadbetter Beach.** Between Santa Barbara Harbor and Shoreline Park, the always active beach is crawling with surfers, swimmers,

One of the many colorful characters you'll find at the Santa Barbara Zoo.

and families enjoying the grassy picnic area. *801 Shoreline Dr. (Loma Alta Dr). Sunrise–10pm.*

⑪ **Brophy Brothers.** It can be noisy and crowded, with sometimes indifferent service, but the super-fresh seafood can't be beat. Ask for an outdoor table to enjoy the harbor view, but if the wait is killing you, don't hesitate to plop down at the bar. Some favorites include the clam chowder, the beer boiled shrimp, and the garlic-baked clams. Consistently voted Best Seafood in Santa Barbara. *119 Harbor Way (in the Waterfront Center), Santa Barbara.* ☎ *805/966-4418. $$.*

Leadbetter Beach.

Santa Catalina Island

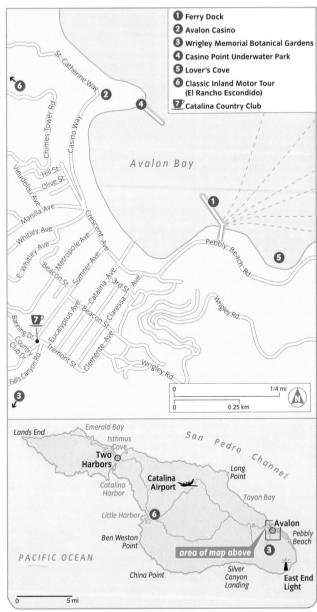

1 Ferry Dock
2 Avalon Casino
3 Wrigley Memorial Botanical Gardens
4 Casino Point Underwater Park
5 Lover's Cove
6 Classic Inland Motor Tour
(El Rancho Escondido)
7 Catalina Country Club

Only 22 miles off the California coast (and still in L.A. County), the island feels like it's across the universe from the hustle-bustle metropolis of Los Angeles. Unspoiled land, clean air, crystal-clear water, and no traffic—a day trip here may feel like a vacation from your vacation. The natural resources are protected by the Santa Catalina Island Conservancy, which owns 88% of the island. Chewing-gum magnate William Wrigley, Jr., purchased the island in 1919 as a remote playground for the exploding population of southern California, and most of what you see today is the result of his vision.

1 Getting There. If you feel like splurging, take a 15-minute helicopter ride over the water and touch down at the helipad near Avalon, the island's only city. The thrilling jaunt provides amazing views of the coastline, and along the way you might spot some whales and dolphins. From 8am until sunset ★★★ **Island Express helicopters** fly out of San Pedro and Long Beach (near the *Queen Mary*). Not recommended for kids or the severely skittish. Most folks opt for the ★ **Catalina Express ferry,** an hour-long ride also departing from San Pedro and Long Beach. Because you'll be taking a round-trip, you can try both air and sea travel. *Island Express helicopters:* ☎ *310/510-2525. www.islandexpress.com. $82 one-way, round-trip $156.*

Reservations required. Catalina Express ferry: Long Beach, San Pedro & Dana Point. ☎ *800/481-3470. www.catalinaexpress.com. Approximately 30 daily departures. One-way: $30 adults, $27 seniors, $23 children; round-trip: $59 adults, $53 seniors, $46 children. Reservations required.*

2 ★★★ Avalon Casino. Wrigley built this multitiered Spanish-Moorish palace in 1929 as an entertainment destination (not for gambling), where big-band legends such as Benny Goodman used to pack crowds at the **Casino Ballroom** in the '30s and '40s. Consider catching a movie at the glamorous **Avalon Theatre** (☎ 310/510-0179), whose walls feature Art Deco murals by John Gabriel Beckman, an artist who

Boats anchored in the Santa Catalina harbor in Avalon.

also worked on Grauman's Chinese Theatre. One of the "newer" attractions (more than 50 years old) is the **Catalina Island Museum** (☎ 310/510-2414), which illustrates 7,000 years of island history with exhibits drawn from over 150,000 items and artifacts. *1 Casino Way, Casino Point. Museum:* ☎ *310/510-2414. Daily 10am–4pm. $4. Theater:* ☎ *310/510-0179. Weekdays at 7pm, weekends 7pm & 9:15pm. $6–$8. Casino Walking Tour:* ☎ *800/626-5440. Daily 10am–4pm. $8–$16, includes free admission to the museum.* www.visitcatalinaisland.com.

❸ **Wrigley Memorial Botanical Gardens.** Take a 1-mile stroll up into Avalon Canyon to see the Romanesque Wrigley Memorial (the views from the tower are splendid) and the 37-acre garden of rare desert plants, many of which are endemic to Catalina. *1400 Avalon Canyon Rd.* ☎ *310/510-2288. Daily*

8am–5pm. $5 adults, free for children under 13.

❹ ★ **Casino Point Underwater Park.** The marine preserve in front of the Casino is an excellent place for scuba diving, and in some places, snorkeling. Rent some equipment and explore the rich marine life surrounding the swaying kelp forests in southern California's first city-designated underwater park. *Catalina Divers Supply:* ☎ *310/510-0330. Daily 8am–4pm during the summer, weekends 8am–4pm in the off-season. $18 for 2-hr. snorkel package, $55 scuba package.*

❺ ★★ **Lover's Cove.** The shallow waters here are ideal for snorkeling; you'll find bright-orange garibaldi, spotted calico bass, sheephead, urchins, rockfish, bat rays, and eels. A drier and more leisurely way to meet the fishes is the **Undersea Tour,** 45 minutes

Visiting Two Harbors

If you want to get a better look at the rugged natural beauty of Catalina and escape the throngs of beachgoers, head over to **Two Harbors,** the quarter-mile "neck" at the island's northwest end that gets its name from the "twin harbors" on each side, known as the Isthmus and Catalina Harbor. An excellent starting point for campers and hikers, Two Harbors also offers just enough civilization for the less-intrepid traveler.

The **Banning House Lodge** (☎ 800/626-1496; www.VisitTwo Harbors.com) is an 11-room bed-and-breakfast overlooking the Isthmus. The clapboard house was built in 1910 for Catalina's pre-Wrigley owners and has seen duty as on-location lodging for movie stars such as Errol Flynn and Dorothy Lamour. Peaceful and isolated, the simply furnished but comfortable lodge has spectacular views of both harbors.

Everyone eats at **The Harbor Reef Restaurant** (☎ 310/510-4215), on the beach. This nautical, tropical-themed saloon/restaurant serves breakfast, lunch, and dinner, the latter consisting of hearty steaks, ribs, swordfish, chicken teriyaki, and buffalo burgers in summer.

The waters in Lover's Cove are a snorkeler's paradise.

⑥ ★★ Classic Inland Motor Tour.

A tour is the only way to fully explore the island's rugged, pristine interior. Traveling along an 1800s stagecoach route in a comfy bus, you'll see American bison (14 were left here for a film shoot in 1925; there are 200 today), Catalina Island foxes, and Arabian horses at the newly remodeled El Rancho Escondido. ☎ 800/626-7489. *$69 adults, $62 seniors, $35 children. Reservations required.*

⑦ Catalina Country Club.

If you normally shy away from meals served in men's locker rooms, maybe you'll reconsider after seeing this elegant restaurant set in a building that served as the Chicago Cubs spring training clubhouse from the early '20s until the early '50s. Try the Clubhouse Bar, which is drenched in nostalgia. *1 Country Club Dr, Avalon.* ☎ 310/510-7404. *$$.*

on a glass-bottom boat. *Lover's Cove Marine Preserve. Undersea Tour: $36 adults, $32 seniors, $18 children.*

The elegant dining room at the Catalina Country Club.

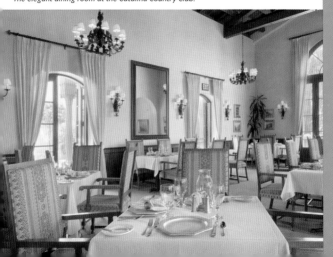

Santa Ynez Wine Country

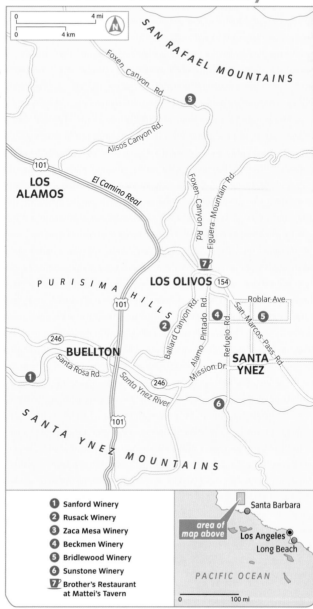

0   4 mi
0   4 km

SAN RAFAEL MOUNTAINS

Foxen Canyon Rd.

③

Alisos Canyon Rd.

101

LOS ALAMOS

El Camino Real

Foxen Canyon Rd.

Figuera Mountain Rd.

PURISIMA HILLS

101

⑦

LOS OLIVOS 154

Roblar Ave.

Ballard Canyon Rd.

Alamo-Pintado Rd.

Refugio Rd.

San Marcos Pass Rd.

②

④

⑤

246

BUELLTON

①

Santa Rosa Rd.

Santa Ynez River

246

Mission Dr.

SANTA YNEZ

⑥

101

SANTA YNEZ MOUNTAINS

① Sanford Winery
② Rusack Winery
③ Zaca Mesa Winery
④ Beckmen Winery
⑤ Bridlewood Winery
⑥ Sunstone Winery
⑦ Brother's Restaurant at Mattei's Tavern

Santa Barbara

area of map above

Los Angeles

Long Beach

PACIFIC OCEAN

0   100 mi

Thirty miles north of Santa Barbara, the Santa Ynez Valley offers an excellent wine country getaway—rolling hills of green vineyards and golden grazing pastures, quaint restaurants, small wineries, and most importantly (perhaps surprisingly), excellent wines, particularly Syrahs and the difficult-to-master pinot noirs. It's no Napa Valley, but that's a good thing; Santa Ynez may not quite have the size and reputation (yet) of Napa Valley, but it also doesn't have the crowds and corporate presence. However, after the success of the Oscar®-nominated movie *Sideways* a few years ago, the valley—which encompasses the towns of Santa Ynez, Los Olivos, Buellton, and Solvang—saw quite an uptick in traffic. *Note:* I do not recommend that you attempt to visit all of these wineries in a single day.

❶ ★ **Sanford Winery.** The winery claims to have planted the first pinot noir in the Santa Rita Hills in 1971 after recognizing a fortuitous combination of climate and soil conditions; it also produces a yummy chardonnay. *Sideways* shot a scene here in the appealingly rustic tasting room, an old dairy barn. *7250 Santa Rosa Rd., Buellton.* ☎ *805/688-3300. Daily 11am–4pm.*

❷ **Rusack Winery.** A boutique winery that produces 5,000 cases a year, Rusack garners stellar reviews for its Syrahs and pinot noirs. If it's warm outside, buy a glass of chilled chardonnay and take a seat on the tree-canopied deck overlooking the vineyards and the oak-dotted hills. *1819 Ballard Canyon Rd., Solvang.* ☎ *805/688-1278. www.rusack.com. Daily 11am–5pm.*

❸ **Zaca Mesa Winery.** The winery focuses on Rhône varietals (Syrah, Grenache, Mourvèdre, Viognier, and Roussanne); their 2005 Viognier has received the most kudos in recent years. Enjoy the scenic 250-acre grounds, which have hiking trails, picnic tables, and a life-size chessboard. *6905 Foxen Canyon Rd., Los Olivos.* ☎ *800/350-7972. www.zacamesa. com. Daily 10am–4pm.*

The barrel barn at the Sanford Winery.

❹ Beckmen Winery. This is a small, family-owned winery with a nifty outdoor deck, a perfect setting for splitting a bottle—maybe an estate-grown Grenache or a small-batch sauvignon blanc—between friends, and taking in the rural beauty. *2670 Ontiveros Rd., Los Olivos.* ☎ *805/688-8664. www.beckmen vineyards.com. Daily 11am–5pm.*

❺ Bridlewood Winery. The winery produces some acclaimed Syrahs, but it's the gorgeous grounds—green and wide open—that produce such a sense of relaxation. *3555 Roblar Ave., Santa Ynez.* ☎ *805/688-9000. www.bridlewood winery.com. Daily 10am–5pm.*

❻ ★★ Sunstone Winery. The winery is designed to make visitors feel as if they've stumbled upon a countryside manor in Provence, and it nearly succeeds. Sunstone is one of the largest organic vineyards in Santa Barbara County, and its tasting room and picnic courtyard are tremendously popular. *125 N. Refugio Rd., Santa Ynez.* ☎ *805/ 688-9463. www.sunstonewinery. com. Daily 10am–4pm.*

Go for a tasting at the Sunstone Winery.

❼ ★★ Brother's Restaurant at Mattei's Tavern. The rambling, clapboard building was built as a stagecoach stop in the 1880s, and it manages to retain all of its Old West history. Their desserts are especially delicious; my favorite is the Brothers' mud pie with Kahlúa-caramel sauce. If it's chilly outside, the coziest seats are the couches in front of the crackling fire. *2350 Railway Ave., Los Olivos.* ☎ *805/688-4820. www.matteistavern.com. $$.* ●

The vineyards and outlying hills of the Zaca Mesa Winery.

The
Savvy Traveler

Before You Go

Tourist Office
Contact **L.A. INC.**, the **Los Angeles Convention & Visitors Bureau,** 685 S. Figueroa St., Los Angeles, CA 90017 (☎ 800/366-6116 or 213/689-8822), for a visitors information kit by mail, or through the website at www.greaterlosangeles.com.

The Best Times to Go
In Los Angeles, as in many places, tourism peaks during **summer.** Hotel rooms and restaurant reservations are harder to come by, and top attractions tend to be packed with both visitors and locals. Although the beach communities almost always remain comfortable, summer can be stifling when daytime temperatures soar and the dreaded L.A. smog is in full effect. Moderate temperatures, fewer crowds, and lower hotel rates make travel to L.A. most enjoyable during the **winter.** From early autumn to late spring, as the smog abates, the city is at its prettiest.

Festivals & Special Events
SPRING. In mid-March to mid-May, the **California Poppy Reserve** in Antelope Valley, less than an hour's drive north of Los Angeles, comes alive in a brilliant display of red and orange. The annual **California Poppy Festival** (☎ 661/723-6077; www.poppyfestival.com) blooms in late April. On weekends from late April to Memorial Day, **Renaissance Pleasure Faire** (☎ 800/52-FAIRE; www.renaissance-faire.com), one of America's largest Renaissance festivals, transforms the Glen Helen Regional Park in San Bernardino into a mystical realm of knights, maidens,

Previous page: Riding in style in Beverly Hills.

dragons, and fairies. Relive the days of yore, if thou wouldst, in period costume. On May 5 and the week surrounding, **Cinco de Mayo** festivities take place in El Pueblo de Los Angeles State Historic Park, Downtown (☎ 213/628-1274). Food, live music, and dancing celebrate the Mexican victory over the French Army in 1862. In the second half of May is the **Venice Art Walk** (☎ 310/392-WALK; www.venicefamilyclinic.org) in Venice Beach. This annual weekend event, nearing its 30th anniversary, leads art lovers on a tour through galleries, and the private home studios of more than 50 established or emerging artists.

SUMMER. In mid-June the **Playboy Jazz Festival** (☎ 213/480-3232) brings top jazz musicians to the Hollywood Bowl. Bill Cosby has presided over ceremonies since 1995. One of the largest lesbian and gay pride festivals and parades in the world, **Christopher Street West Festival & Parade** (☎ 323/969-8302; www.lapride.org) takes place in West Hollywood in the first half of June. There's food, music, dancing, general fabulousness, and then more dancing, all of which culminates in a parade down Santa Monica Boulevard on Sunday. Across 10 days in late June and early July, the well-attended **Los Angeles Film Festival** (☎ 866/345-6337; www.lafilmfest.com) showcases more than 175 American and international indies, and short films. Surf's up in early August for the **International Surf Festival** (www.surffestival.org), which takes place in Hermosa Beach, Manhattan Beach, and Redondo Beach. Other contests include soccer, volleyball, running, swimming, and sand-castle building. In mid-August, celebrate

Japanese culture and heritage at the **Nisei Week Japanese Festival** (☎ 213/687-7193; www.nisei week.org) in Little Tokyo. Festivities include parades, food, Taiko Drum performances, arts, and crafts.

FALL. One of the largest county fairs in the world, **Los Angeles County Fair** (☎ 909/623-3111; www.la countyfair.com) takes place throughout September at the Los Angeles County Fair and Exposition Center in Pomona. Attractions include concerts, carnival rides, horse racing, food contests, arts and crafts, agricultural displays, and educational exhibitions. Over 2 consecutive long weekends in early October, the popular **Catalina Island Jazz Trax Festival** (☎ 760/323-1171; www. jazztrax.com) offers performances by contemporary jazz greats at Avalon's legendary Casino Ballroom. The **Halloween Carnaval** (☎ 310/ 289-2525; www.weho.org) in West Hollywood is one of the world's largest Halloween parties with hundreds of thousands of insanely costumed people partying all night along Santa Monica Boulevard on October 31. In early November **American Film Institute's AFI Fest** (☎ 866/AFI-FEST; www.afi fest.com), going strong after 20 years, gathers some of the biggest names in the international film community to present new movies from around the globe.

WINTER. Every January 1, the world-famous **Tournament of Roses** (☎ 626/449-4100; www.tournament ofroses.com) parades down Colorado Boulevard in Pasadena with spectacular floats, precise marching bands, and colorful equestrian entries. The Rose Bowl football game plays immediately afterward. In early February, celebrate the **Chinese New Year** at the **Golden Dragon Parade** in Chinatown. Dragon dancers and martial-arts

masters take to the streets with 2 dozen floats and several marching bands. For more info, contact the Chinese Chamber of Commerce (☎ 213/617-0396; www.lagolden dragonparade.com). In mid-February the PGA Tour comes to the beautiful and historic Riviera Country Club in Pacific Palisades for the **Nissan Open.** Look for celebrity faces in the crowd. For more info, contact the Los Angeles Junior Chamber of Commerce (☎ 213/ 482-1311; www.lajcc.org). During the first weekend in March, the **Los Angeles Marathon** (☎ 310/444-5544; www.lamarathon.com) draws thousands of participants and a million spectators. The run starts in Downtown Los Angeles, where there's also a 5K Run/Walk.

Weather
People sometimes think of L.A. as perpetually sunny and mild, but it does have a couple of unique seasons: "June Gloom" and "the Santa Anas." "June Gloom" refers to the ocean fog that keeps the beach communities (and often the whole city) overcast into early afternoon; it's most common in June but can occur any time between March and mid-August. The "Santa Anas" are strong, hot winds that race into town from across the desert in the middle of autumn. The winds increase brush-fire danger (and, on the plus side, good offshore conditions for surfing). Aside from these minor disturbances, Los Angeles averages nearly 300 days of sunny skies per year, with an average mean temperature of 66°F (19°C). You can sunbathe throughout the year, but you'll need a wetsuit to venture into the ocean in winter, when water temps hover around 50° to 55°F (10°–13°C). In the summer and fall, the water usually warms to about 65° to 70°F

Useful Websites

- **www.la.com**: This comprehensive website contains the most up-to-date info on L.A. shopping, dining, entertainment, gossip, and nightlife. If it's not here, it's not happening.
- **www.calendarlive.com**: From the *L.A. Times,* Calendar Live is loaded with entertainment, nightlife, and cultural reviews, as well as specialty guides for Disney, Universal Studios, and more.
- **www.laweekly.com**: The online edition of the alternative *L.A. Weekly* paper combines listings with social commentary. It has an events calendar, arts listings and critiques, and restaurant reviews from Pulitzer Prize–winning Jonathan Gold.
- **http://losangeles.citysearch.com**: The local City Search site features movie/sports/entertainment listings, as well as user-driven recommendations and reviews.
- **www.losangeles.com**: From Boulevards New Media, this site emphasizes travel, arts, entertainment, contemporary culture, and politics.

(18°–21°C), which some still find to be too chilly. Los Angeles averages about 34 days of rainfall a year (usually Feb–Apr); this isn't much, but it can cause flooding when it strikes fast. Rain is extremely rare between May and November.

Cellphones

Most likely your phone will work fine in L.A., but to be safe, confirm with your wireless company's coverage map on its website before leaving home. It's also possible to **rent** a phone from **InTouch USA** (☎ 800/872-7626; www.intouchglobal.com). At the arrival level of the international terminal at LAX airport, visitors can find a rental kiosk for a phone-rental company called **TripTel.** Phones can be dropped off at the airport or shipped back via Federal Express when you're done. For more information, call ☎ 877/TRIP-TEL or log on to www.triptel.com.

Car Rental

Los Angeles is one of the cheapest places in America to rent a car. Major national car-rental companies usually rent economy- and compact-class cars for about $35 per day and $120 per week, with unlimited mileage. All the major car-rental agencies have offices at the airport and in the larger hotels. Some of the national car-rental companies that have offices in Los Angeles include **Alamo** (☎ 800/462-5266; www.alamo.com), **Avis** (☎ 800/230-4898; www.avis.com), **Budget** (☎ 800/527-0700; www.budget.com), **Dollar** (☎ 800/800-3665; www.dollar.com), **Hertz** (☎ 800/654-3131; www.hertz.com), **National** (☎ 800/227-7368; www.nationalcar.com), and **Thrifty** (☎ 800/847-4389; www.thrifty.com).

Getting **There**

By Plane

Five airports serve the Los Angeles area. Most visitors fly into **Los Angeles International Airport** (☎ 310/646-5252; www.lawa.org/lax), better known as LAX, which is situated oceanside, between Marina del Rey and Manhattan Beach. LAX is a convenient place to land; it's located within minutes of Santa Monica and the beaches, and not more than a half-hour from Downtown, Hollywood, and the Westside. Free shuttle buses connect the terminals and stop in front of each ticket building. Special minibuses accessible to travelers with disabilities are also available.

For some travelers, one of the area's smaller airports might be more convenient than LAX. **Bob Hope Airport** (2627 N. Hollywood Way, Burbank; ☎ 818/840-8840; www.bobhopeairport.com) is especially easy to use and is accessible to the valley, Hollywood, and Downtown L.A. **Long Beach Municipal Airport** (4100 Donald Douglas Dr., Long Beach; ☎ 562/570-2600; www.lgb.org), south of LAX, is the best place to land if you're visiting Long Beach or northern Orange County and want to avoid L.A. **John Wayne Airport** (19051 Airport Way N., Anaheim; ☎ 949/252-5200; www.ocair.com) is closest to Disneyland, Knott's Berry Farm, and other Orange County attractions. **Ontario International Airport** (Terminal Way, Ontario; ☎ 909/937-2700; www.lawa.org/ont) is not a popular airport for tourists; businesspeople use it to head to San Bernardino, Riverside, and other inland communities. It can also be convenient for going to Palm Springs.

GETTING TO & FROM THE AIRPORT   By Taxi: Expect to pay about $35 to Hollywood and Downtown, $25 to Beverly Hills, $20 to Santa Monica, and $45 to $60 to the Valley and Pasadena, including a $2.50 service charge for rides originating at LAX.

By Shuttle: Many city hotels provide free shuttles for their guests; ask when you make reservations. **SuperShuttle** (☎ 800/258-3826 or 310/782-6600; www.supershuttle.com) offers regularly scheduled minivans from LAX to any location in the city.

By Car

Los Angeles is accessible by many major highways. If you're coming **from the north,** you can take the quick route along I-5 through the middle of the state, or the scenic route along the coast. To reach the beach communities and L.A.'s Westside, take I-405 south, which is notorious for heavy, slow-moving traffic; to get to Hollywood, take California 170 south to U.S. 101 south (this route is called Hollywood Fwy. the entire way); I-5 will take you along the eastern edge of Downtown and into Orange County.

If you're taking the **scenic coastal route** from the north, take U.S. 101 to I-405 or I-5, or stay on U.S. 101, following the instructions above to your destination. If you're approaching **from the east,** you'll be coming in on I-10. For Orange County, take California 57 south. I-10 continues through Downtown and terminates at the beach. If you're heading to the Westside, take I-405 north. To get to the beaches, take California 1 (PCH) north or south, depending on your destination. **From the south,** head north on I-5 at the southern end of Orange County. I-405 splits off to the west;

take this road to the Westside and beach communities. Stay on I-5 to reach Downtown and Hollywood.

By Train

Amtrak (☎ 800/USA-RAIL; www. amtrakcalifornia.com) connects Los Angeles with about 500 American cities. The L.A. train terminus is **Union Station,** 800 N. Alameda (☎ 213/617-0111), on Downtown's northern edge.

Getting **Around**

By Car

L.A.'s urban sprawl is connected by an elaborate network of well-maintained freeways, so a car is the best way to get around. The system works well to get you where you need to be, although rush-hour (roughly 6–9am and 3–7pm) traffic is often bumper-to-bumper, particularly on the congested I-405.

By Taxi

Typically, distances are long in Los Angeles, and cab fares can run high, even for a short trip. It's possible to hail a cab when you're Downtown, but everywhere else you'll need to order a taxi in advance from **Checker Cab** (☎ 323/654-8400), **L.A. Taxi** (☎ 213/627-7000), or **United Taxi** (☎ 213/483-7604).

By Public Transportation

It's possible, but certainly not preferable, to tour Los Angeles entirely by public transportation. The metropolis is most navigable by automobile; many areas are simply inaccessible without one. Public transport might work for you if you're in the city for only a short time, are on a very tight budget, or don't expect to be moving around a lot. The city's trains and buses are operated by the **Los Angeles County Metropolitan Transit Authority** (MTA; ☎ 213/922-2000; www.mta. net), and MTA brochures and schedules are available at every area visitor center.

By Bus: Extensive touring by bus is simply not practical; stops are too spread out, and transfers are too frequent. For short trips, buses remain an economical and environmentally correct choice. However, riding buses late at night should be avoided. The basic bus fare is $1.25 for all local lines, with transfers costing 25¢. A **Metro Day Pass** is $3 and gives you unlimited bus and rail rides all day; these can be purchased while boarding any Metro Bus (exact change is needed) or at the self-service vending machines at the Metro Rail stations. The **Downtown Area Short Hop (DASH)** shuttle system operates buses throughout Downtown, Hollywood, and the Westside. Service runs every 5 to 20 minutes, depending on the time of day, and costs just 25¢. Contact the Department of Transportation (☎ 213/808-2273; www.ladottransit.com) for schedules and route information. The **Cityline** shuttle is a great way to get around West Hollywood on weekdays (9am–4pm) and Saturday (10am–7:30pm). For 50¢, it'll take you to most of the major shops and restaurants throughout WeHo (very handy if you park your car in a flat-fee lot). For more information, call ☎ 800/447-2189.

By Rail & Subway: L.A.'s subway system does not serve the entire city. The **Metro Blue Line,** an aboveground rail line, connects

Downtown Los Angeles with Long Beach. Trains operate daily from 6am to 9pm; the fare is $1.25. The **Metro Red Line** begins at Union Station, the city's main train depot, and travels west underneath Wilshire Boulevard, looping north into Hollywood and the San Fernando Valley. The fare is $1.25; discount tokens are available at Metro service centers and many area convenience stores. The **Metro Purple Line** subway shares six stations with the Red Line Downtown and continues to the Mid-Wilshire area. The fare is $1.25. The **Metro Green Line** runs for 20 miles along the center of the new I-105, the Glenn Anderson (Century) Freeway, and

connects Norwalk in eastern Los Angeles County to LAX. A connection with the Blue Line offers visitors access from LAX to Downtown L.A. or Long Beach. The fare is $1.25. The **Metro Gold Line** is a 14-mile link between Pasadena and Union Station in Downtown L.A. Stops include Old Pasadena, the Southwest Museum, and Chinatown. The fare is $1.25. Weekly Metro passes are available for $14 at Metro Customer Centers and local convenience and grocery stores. For more information on public transportation call **MTA** at ☎ 213/922-2000, or, better yet, log on to their handy website at www.mta.net.

Fast **Facts**

AREA CODES   Areas west of La Cienega Boulevard, including Beverly Hills and the city's beach communities, use the **310** area code. Portions of Los Angeles County east and south of the city, including Long Beach, are in the **562** area. The San Fernando Valley has the **818** area code, while points east—including parts of Burbank, Glendale, and Pasadena—use the newly created **626** code. The Downtown business area uses **213.** All other numbers, including Griffith Park, Hollywood, and parts of West Hollywood (east of La Cienega Blvd.), use area code **323.**

ATMS/CASHPOINTS   The **Cirrus** (☎ 800/424-7787; www.mastercard.com) and **PLUS** (☎ 800/843-7587; www.visa.com) networks span the globe; look at the back of your bankcard to see which network you're on, and then call or check online for ATM locations. Find out your daily withdrawal limit before you depart.

BABYSITTERS   If you're staying at one of the larger hotels, the concierge can usually recommend a reliable babysitter. If not, contact the **Baby-Sitters Guild** in Glendale (☎ 310/837-1800 or 818/552-2229), L.A.'s oldest and largest babysitting service.

BANKS   Most banks are open weekdays from 9am to 5pm and sometimes Saturday mornings. Many banks have ATMs for 24-hour banking.

BUSINESS HOURS   Offices are usually open weekdays from 9am to 5pm. Stores typically open between 9 and 10am and close between 5 and 6pm from Monday through Saturday. Stores in shopping complexes or malls tend to stay open late, until about 9pm, and many malls and larger department stores are open on Sundays.

DENTISTS   For a recommendation in the area, call the **Dental Referral Service** (☎ 800/422-8338).

DOCTORS   See "Hospital," below.

DRINKING LAWS   The legal age for purchase and consumption of alcoholic beverages is 21; proof of age is required and often requested at bars, nightclubs, and restaurants, so it's always a good idea to bring ID when you go out. Do not carry open containers of alcohol in your car or any public area that isn't zoned for alcohol consumption. The police can fine you on the spot. And nothing will ruin your trip faster than getting a citation for DUI ("driving under the influence"), so don't even think about driving while intoxicated.

DRUGSTORES & PHARMACIES   Contact **Walgreens** (☎ 800/WALGREEN; www.walgreens.com) or **Rite-Aid** (☎ 800/RITE-AID; www.riteaid.com) for a location near you.

ELECTRICITY   Like Canada, the United States uses 110–120 volts AC (60 cycles), compared to 220–240 volts AC (50 cycles) in most of Europe, Australia, and New Zealand. If your small appliances use 220–240 volts, you'll need a 110-volt transformer and a plug adapter with two flat, parallel pins to operate them here. Downward converters that change 220–240 volts to 110–120 volts are difficult to find in the United States, so bring one with you.

EMBASSIES & CONSULATES   All embassies are located in the nation's capital, Washington, D.C. Some consulates are located in major U.S. cities, and most nations have a mission to the United Nations in New York City. For a directory of embassies in Washington, D.C., call ☎ 202/555-1212 or log on to www.embassy.org/embassies. The embassy of **Australia** is at 1601 Massachusetts Ave. NW, Washington, DC 20036 (☎ 202/797-3000; www.austemb.org); the embassy of **Canada** is at 501 Pennsylvania Ave. NW, Washington, DC 20001 (☎ 202/682-1740;

www.canadianembassy.org); the embassy of **Ireland** is at 2234 Massachusetts Ave. NW, Washington, DC 20008 (☎ 202/462-3939; www.irelandemb.org); the embassy of **New Zealand** is at 37 Observatory Circle NW, Washington, DC 20008 (☎ 202/328-4800; www.nzemb.org); the embassy of the **United Kingdom** is at 3100 Massachusetts Ave. NW, Washington, DC 20008 (☎ 202/588-7800; www.britainusa.com).

EMERGENCIES   Call ☎ 911 to report a fire, call the police, or get an ambulance anywhere in the United States. The **Poison Control Center** can be reached ☎ 800/222/1222, toll free from any phone. If you encounter traveler's problems, call the Los Angeles chapter of the **Traveler's Aid Society** (☎ 310/646-2270; www.travelersaid.org), a nationwide, nonprofit, social service organization that helps travelers in difficult straits.

GAY & LESBIAN TRAVEL RESOURCES   Two great resources for L.A.'s gay and lesbian visitors are the **L.A. Gay and Lesbian Center** (☎ 323/993-7400; www.laglc.org), an advocacy group; and the **West Hollywood Convention and Visitors Bureau** (☎ 800/368-6020; www.gogaywesthollywood.com), which provides info on everything from events to accommodations.

HOLIDAYS   Banks, government offices, post offices, and many stores, restaurants, and museums are closed on the following legal national holidays: January 1 (New Year's Day), the third Monday in January (Martin Luther King, Jr., Day), the third Monday in February (Presidents' Day), the last Monday in May (Memorial Day), July 4th (Independence Day), the first Monday in September (Labor Day), the second Monday in October (Columbus Day), November 11 (Veterans Day/

Armistice Day), the fourth Thursday in November (Thanksgiving Day), and December 25 (Christmas). The Tuesday after the first Monday in November is Election Day, a federal government holiday in presidential-election years (held every 4 years, and next in 2008).

HOSPITAL   The centrally located **Cedars-Sinai Medical Center,** 8700 Beverly Blvd., Los Angeles (☎ 310/423-3277), has a 24-hour emergency room staffed by some of the country's finest MDs.

INSURANCE   The cost of travel insurance varies widely, depending on the cost and length of your trip, your age and health, and the type of trip you're taking, but expect to pay between 5% and 8% of the vacation itself. You can get estimates from various providers through **Insure-MyTrip.com.** Enter your trip cost and dates, your age, and other information, for prices from more than a dozen companies. **Trip-cancellation insurance** will help retrieve your money if you have to back out of a trip or depart early, or if your travel supplier goes bankrupt. You won't get back 100% of your prepaid trip cost, but you'll be refunded a substantial portion. **TravelSafe** (☎ 888/885-7233; www.travelsafe.com) offers coverage. **Expedia.com** also offers any-reason cancellation coverage for its air-hotel packages.

Although it's not required of travelers, **health insurance** is highly recommended. International visitors should note that unlike many European countries, the U.S. does not usually offer free or low-cost medical care to its citizens or visitors. Doctors and hospitals are expensive and, in most cases, will require advance payment or proof of insurance coverage before they will render their services. Though lack of insurance may prevent you from

being admitted to a hospital in non-emergencies, don't worry about being left on a street corner to die: The American way is to fix you now and bill the living daylights out of you later.

For **lost luggage** on flights within the U.S., checked baggage is covered up to $2,500 per ticketed passenger. On flights outside the U.S. (and on U.S. portions of international trips), baggage coverage is limited to approximately $9.07 per pound, up to approximately $635 per checked bag. If you plan to check items more valuable than what's covered by the standard liability, see if your homeowner's policy covers your valuables, get baggage insurance as part of your comprehensive travel-insurance package, or buy Travel Guard's "Bag-Trak" product. If your luggage is lost, immediately file a lost-luggage claim at the airport, detailing the luggage contents. Most airlines require that you report delayed, damaged, or lost baggage within 4 hours of arrival. The airlines are required to deliver luggage, once found, directly to your house or destination free of charge.

INTERNET ACCESS   **Cyber Java** (☎ 323/466-5600) is conveniently located at 7080 Hollywood Blvd. (near La Brea Ave.). You can also get online at public libraries such as the one at 161 S. Gardner St., near the Grove. Go to www.lapl.org to find more locations.

Most major airports have Internet kiosks that provide basic Web access for a per-minute fee that's usually higher than cybercafe prices. Check out copy shops like Kinko's (FedEx Kinko's), which offers computer stations with fully loaded software (as well as Wi-Fi). Most laptops sold today have built-in wireless capability. To find public Wi-Fi hotspots at your destination, go to www.jiwire.com; its Hotspot Finder holds the world's largest directory of public wireless hotspots. Many Starbucks locations are T-Mobile hotspots; you can purchase hourly, daily, or monthly passes.

MAIL   Domestic rates are 26¢ for a postcard and 41¢ for a letter. For international mail, a first-class letter of up to 1 ounce costs 90¢ (69¢ to Canada and Mexico); a first-class postcard costs the same as a letter. The main post office is located at 7101 S. Central Ave., Los Angeles, CA 90001; it's open Monday to Friday 7am to 7pm and Saturday 7am to 3:30pm.

NEWSPAPERS & MAGAZINES   The *Los Angeles Times* (www.latimes.com) is a high-quality daily with strong local and national coverage. Its Sunday "Calendar" section (www.calendar live.com) is an excellent guide to entertainment. The *L.A. Weekly* (www.laweekly.com), a free weekly listings magazine, is packed with information on current events around town.

PASSPORTS   Always keep a copy of your passport with you when you're traveling. If your passport is lost or stolen, having a copy significantly facilitates the reissuing process at a local consulate or embassy. Keep your passport and other valuables in your room's safe or in the hotel safe. See "Embassies & Consulates," above, for more information.

POLICE   In an emergency, dial ☎ 911. For non-emergency police matters, call ☎ 213/485-2121; in Beverly Hills, dial ☎ 310/550-4951.

PARKING   There are some frustrating parts of town (particularly around restaurants after 7:30pm) where you might have to give in and use valet parking. Restaurants and nightclubs usually charge between $3 and $6. Some areas, like Santa Monica and Beverly Hills, offer self-park

lots and garages near the neighborhood action; costs range from $2 to $10. Also, have plenty of quarters for meters and read posted restrictions carefully.

SMOKING   California law prohibits smoking in public buildings, restaurants, and bars. Many hotels are completely nonsmoking, and others have limited floors for smokers.

TAXES   Sales tax in Los Angeles is 8%. Hotel tax is charged on the room tariff only (which is not subject to sales tax) and is set by the city, ranging from 12% to 17% around southern California.

TELEPHONES   For local directory assistance ("information"), dial ☎ 411; for long-distance information, dial 1, then the appropriate area code, and ☎ 555-1212. Most long-distance and international calls can be dialed directly from any phone.

TIPPING   In hotels, tip **bellhops** at least $1 per bag and tip the **chamber staff** $1 to $2 per day (more if you've left a disaster area). Tip the **doorman** or **concierge** only if he or she has provided you with some specific service (for example, calling a cab for you or obtaining difficult-to-get theater tickets). Tip the **valet-parking attendant** $1 every time you get your car. In restaurants, bars, and nightclubs, **service staff** expect 15% to 20% of the check, **bartenders** 10% to 15%, **check-room attendants** $1 per garment, and **valet-parking attendants** $1 per vehicle. Tip **cabdrivers** 15%, **skycaps** at airports at least $1 per bag, and **hairdressers** and **barbers** 15% to 20%.

TOILETS   You won't find public toilets or "restrooms" on the streets of L.A., but they can be found in hotel lobbies, bars, restaurants, museums, department stores, railway and bus stations, and service stations. Large hotels and fast-food restaurants are often the best bet for clean facilities.

TOURIST INFORMATION   The **Los Angeles Convention and Visitors Bureau (L.A. INC.;** ☎ 800/366-6116 or 213/689-8822; www.visitLAnow.com) is the city's main source for information. The bureau provides two **walk-in visitor centers:** Downtown at 685 S. Figueroa St. (Mon–Fri 9am–5pm), and in Hollywood at the Hollywood & Highland Center, 6801 Hollywood Blvd. (daily 10am–11pm).

WEATHER   Call **Los Angeles Weather Information (**☎ 213/554-1212) for the daily forecast. For beach conditions, call the **Zuma Beach Lifeguard** recorded information (☎ 310/457-9701).

A Brief **History**

1542 Juan Cabrillo, a Portuguese explorer, claims the area as the City of God for the Spanish Empire, but does not establish a settlement.

1771 Franciscan friar Junípero Serra leads the establishment of the Mission San Gabriel Arcangel near present-day San Gabriel Valley.

1781 A multicultural group of 44 settlers, under orders from Spanish governor Felipe de Neve, establish "El Pueblo de Nuestra Señora la Reina de los Angeles del Río de Porciúncula" near present-day Olvera Street.

1822 Mexico achieves its independence from the Spanish Empire and claims Los Angeles and the rest of California.

1848 After 3 years of skirmishes, the U.S.-Mexican Treaty gives California to the United States.

1850 California becomes the 31st state of the union, and the City of Los Angeles is incorporated with a population of just over 1,500.

1885 The transcontinental railroad reaches Los Angeles, and southern California experiences its first land boom.

1892 Oil is discovered in Los Angeles by Edward L. Doheny.

1903 Hollywood is incorporated. The conservative community forbids the sale of alcohol.

1911 The Nestor Film Company, Hollywood's first film studio, takes over a tavern at Sunset and Gower boulevards.

1914 In a barn near Hollywood and Vine, Samuel Goldwyn, Cecil B. DeMille, and Jesse Lasky make the first feature-length film, *The Squaw Man*.

1923 The city produces a quarter of the world's petroleum.

1923 A large sign that reads HOLLYWOODLAND is erected on Mount Lee as an advertisement for a Hollywood Hills housing development.

1927 Grauman's Chinese Theatre opens in Hollywood by showing Cecil B. DeMille's *The King of Kings*.

1929 The first Academy Awards ceremony takes place in the Blossom Room of the Hollywood Roosevelt Hotel.

1932 The city hosts the Summer Olympics for the first time. Population tops one million people.

1940 A highway between Los Angeles and Pasadena opens. The success of the Arroyo Seco Parkway convinces Angelenos that an elaborate freeway system could be the solution to the region's transportation problems.

1955 Crowds start lining up at 2am on July 18 for the public opening of Disneyland.

1958 Having moved from Brooklyn, the Los Angeles Dodgers play their first game in their new hometown, in front of nearly 80,000 fans at the Los Angeles Memorial Coliseum.

1965 Race riots rage in Watts for 6 days, causing 34 deaths and $35 million in damages.

1967 Former actor Ronald Reagan is elected governor of California.

1968 Robert Kennedy is assassinated at the Ambassador Hotel shortly after declaring victory in California's Democratic primary.

1973 Tom Bradley is elected mayor and holds the office for 20 years. At the time he's only the second African American elected mayor of a major U.S. city.

1984 Los Angeles hosts the Summer Olympics for the second time.

1988 Kirk Gibson's dramatic home run wins Game 1 of the World Series, which the Dodgers go on to win in five games.

1992 Race riots sparked by the Rodney King verdict result in approximately 50 deaths, 2,000 people injured, 10,000 people arrested, and material damages estimated between $800 million and $1 billion.

1994 The 6.7 Northridge earthquake shakes the city, causing 72 deaths and an estimated $12.5 billion in damage, making it one of the costliest natural disasters in U.S. history.

1995 A jury acquits O.J. Simpson of the double homicide of Nicole Brown Simpson and Ronald Goldman.

1997 The Getty Center opens.

1999–2000 Los Angeles Lakers Shaquille O'Neal and Kobe Bryant team up for the first of three NBA Championships in a row.

2001 The Academy Awards ceremony moves into its permanent residence at the Kodak Theatre in Hollywood.

2003 Former actor Arnold Schwarzenegger is elected governor of California.

2007 A wildfire burns more than 817 acres in Griffith Park, destroying the bird sanctuary, Dante's View, and Captain's Roost.

Los Angeles in Film

Billy Wilder's *Double Indemnity* (1944)
Billy Wilder's *Sunset Boulevard* (1950)
Nicholas Ray's *Rebel Without a Cause* (1955)

Roman Polanski's *Chinatown* (1974)
Ridley Scott's *Blade Runner* (1982)
Martha Coolidge's *Valley Girl* (1983)
Garry Marshall's *Pretty Woman* (1990)
Mick Jackson's *L.A. Story* (1991)

John Singleton's *Boyz n the Hood* (1991)
Robert Altman's *The Player* (1992)
Doug Liman's *Swingers* (1996)

Curtis Hanson's *L.A. Confidential* (1997)
David Lynch's *Mulholland Drive* (2001)

Toll-Free Numbers & Websites

Airlines

AER LINGUS
☎ 800/474-7424
☎ 3531/886-8844 in Ireland
www.aerlingus.ie

AIR CANADA
☎ 888/247-2262
www.aircanada.com

AIRTRAN AIRLINES
☎ 800/247-8726
www.airtran.com

AMERICAN AIRLINES
☎ 800/433-7300
www.aa.com

AMERICA WEST AIRLINES
☎ 800/235-9292
www.americawest.com

ATA AIRLINES
☎ 800/225-2995
www.ata.com

BRITISH AIRWAYS
☎ 800/247-9297
☎ 0870/850-9850 in the U.K.
www.british-airways.com

CONTINENTAL AIRLINES
☎ 800/525-0280
www.continental.com

DELTA AIR LINES
☎ 800/221-1212
www.delta.com

JETBLUE AIRWAYS
☎ 800/538-2583
www.jetblue.com

MIDWEST
☎ 800/452-2022
www.midwestexpress.com

NORTHWEST AIRLINES
☎ 800/225-2525
www.nwa.com

UNITED AIRLINES
☎ 800/241-6522
www.ual.com

US AIRWAYS
☎ 800/428-4322
www.usairways.com

VIRGIN ATLANTIC AIRWAYS
☎ 800/821-5438
☎ 0870/380-2007 in the U.K.
www.virgin-atlantic.com

Car-Rental Agencies

ALAMO
☎ 800/462-5266
www.alamo.com

AVIS
☎ 800/831-1212
www.avis.com

BUDGET
☎ 800/527-0700
www.budget.com

DOLLAR
☎ 800/800-3665
www.dollar.com

ENTERPRISE
☎ 800/261-7331
www.enterprise.com

HERTZ
☎ 800/654-3131
www.hertz.com

NATIONAL
☎ 800/227-7368
www.nationalcar.com

THRIFTY
☎ 800/847-4389
www.thrifty.com

Index

See also Accommodations and Restaurant indexes, below.

Index

Photo **Credits**

The new way to get AROUND town.

Make the most of your stay. Go Day by Day.

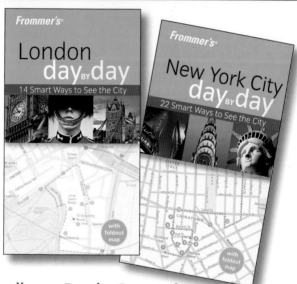

Frommer's® **London** day BY day
14 Smart Ways to See the City
with foldout map

Frommer's® **New York City** day BY day
22 Smart Ways to See the City
with foldout map

The all-new Day by Day series shows you the best places to visit and the best way to see them.

- Full-color throughout, with hundreds of photos and maps
- Packed with 1–to–3–day itineraries, neighborhood walks, and thematic tours
- Museums, literary haunts, offbeat places, and more
- Star-rated hotel and restaurant listings
- Sturdy foldout map in reclosable plastic wallet
- Foldout front covers with at-a-glance maps and info

The best trips start here. **Frommer's®**